Series / Number 07-005

LF

COHORT ANALYSIS

NORVAL D. GLENN
University of Texas

⑤ SAGE PUBLICATIONS / Beverly Hills / London

For information address:

SAGE PUBLICATIONS, INC.
275 South Beverly Drive
Beverly Hills, California 90212

SAGE PUBLICATIONS LTD
28 Banner Street
London EC1Y 8QE, England

International Standard Book Number 0-8039-0794-X

Library of Congress Catalog Card No. L.C. 77-75942

SECOND PRINTING

When citing a University Paper, please use the proper form. Remember to cite the
correct Sage University Paper series title and include the paper number. One of the
two following formats can be adapted (depending on the style manual used):

(1) IVERSEN, GUDMUND R. and NORPOTH, HELMUT (1976) "Analysis of
Variance." Sage University Paper series on Quantitative Applications in the Social
Sciences, 07-001. Beverly Hills and London: Sage Pubns.

OR

(2) Iversen, Gudmund R. and Norpoth, Helmut. 1976. *Analysis of Variance.* Sage
University Paper series on Quantitative Applications in the Social Sciences, series no.
07-001. Beverly Hills and London: Sage Publications.

CONTENTS

NORVAL D. GLENN, professor of sociology at the University of Texas at Austin, has served in editorial capacities for such publications as Social Science Quarterly, American Sociological Review, *and* Public Opinion Quarterly. *He is editor-designate of* Contemporary Sociology. *Dr. Glenn did his undergraduate work at New Mexico State University and earned his Ph.D. at the University of Texas at Austin. In addition to numerous articles in professional journals, Dr. Glenn has coauthored several books:* Transformation of the Negro American *(1965),* Blacks in the United States: An Anthology *(1969), and* Social Stratification: A Research Bibliography *(1970).*

Editor's Introduction

The word *generation* is frequently misused. Technically it is a structural term derived from the parent-child relationship and should be reserved to that usage. Its other common use—to identify a group of individuals who are linked by age (the "Depression babies") or modes (the "Pepsi generation") or class (law students)—is correctly an identification of *cohorts*. A cohort is any group of individuals linked as a group in some way—usually by age. And COHORT ANALYSIS is a method for investigating the changes in patterns of behavior or attitudes of such groups.

This paper demonstrates the application of COHORT ANALYSIS by analyzing these three types of changes:

(1) actual changes in the behavior or attitudes of a cohort,

(2) changes that can be attributed to the process of the aging of the cohort,

(3) changes which are associated with the events of a particular period (for example, the effect of the Great Depression of the 1930s or the effect of the Watergate happenings on a particular population).

COHORT ANALYSIS is a method for analyzing such changes through the use of a wide-ranging set of statistical techniques described in this paper. The critical problem is the identification of the cohort and the design of a research program to determine which of the three types of change listed above is dominant as the group modifies its behavior and attitudes. For example, this paper analyzes changing survey responses to the question of admission of mainland China to the United Nations, and it studies non-Catholic responses over time to the possibility of a Catholic president. These studies illustrate the importance of COHORT ANALYSIS in that they allow inferences about changing patterns of behavior within a subgroup—without the need to requestion the same individuals at different points in time.

Unlike the other papers in this series, COHORT ANALYSIS presupposes no specific background in a particular type of data analysis and it is not in itself a statistical technique. Instead it is a highly flexible tool of great practical utility to social science researchers:

● Sociologists might use COHORT ANALYSIS to learn if changes in friendship groups result from exposure to new people, changes of attitudes within a cohort, or such other factors as increased education or economic status. The problem in such a study would be to identify changing cohorts over time as the reference groups for the individuals change.

- Political scientists might use COHORT ANALYSIS to inquire whether members of a legislative body tend to display similar voting patterns as their careers progress. Or do such cohort effects, clearly noticeable in members' first terms, dissipate as the individual members are influenced by state party delegations or committee assignments? Do American voters increase the strength of their identification with a political party on the basis of their individual place in the life-cycle (that is, older voters are more likely to vote for the Republican party) or on the basis of the length of time that the individual has been loyal to a particular party (that is, once a Democrat, always a Democrat).*

- Psychologists and educators might use COHORT ANALYSIS to determine if there is a similar pattern of learning behavior among students who remain in the same cohort (class group) in school. Do learning patterns hold constant regardless of the quality of teacher assigned to the class—and do the patterns alter if the cohort is dispersed into alternative groupings?

- Economists might use COHORT ANALYSIS to explore the possibility that rates of economic growth of various nations are a function of such cohort similarities as time of independence; alternatively, they might compare the effects on a cohort of nations of a variety of economic systems, particularly differentiated by the extent to which government becomes involved in the economy.

Since any group is a cohort, any group that experiences change can be a subject for COHORT ANALYSIS. This paper discusses the technique of COHORT ANALYSIS—not so much to tell you how to do it, but rather to tell you how to find the questions to pose in conducting such an analysis.

—E. M. Uslaner, Series Editor

---

*For a complete treatment of party identification studies, see the book by Philip E. Converse (1976) *The Dynamics of Party Support: Cohort-Analyzing Party Identification.* Sage Library of Social Research, vol. 35. Beverly Hills and London: Sage Publications.

COHORT ANALYSIS

NORVAL D. GLENN
University of Texas

INTRODUCTION

Cohort analysis is a method of research developed by demographers and for many years applied primarily to the study of fertility. In recent years, it has been adapted to the study of various attitudinal and behavioral phenomena and especially to the study of such political phenomena as voter turnout and party identification. More broadly, it has become extolled as a technique with great potential for providing insight into the effects of human aging and into the nature of social, cultural, and political change. Although its potential is not as great as its most enthusiastic proponents and practitioners have believed, it is undoubtedly a useful technique (or, more accurately, a number of related techniques) destined to become more widely used as vast amounts of survey sample data appropriate for cohort studies accumulate in the data archives. To an increasing extent, social scientific researchers concerned with aging and with social, cultural, and political change must understand the terminology, logic, and rudimentary principles of cohort analysis to be considered competent; most will sooner or later find occasion to conduct cohort analyses or to use in their research the findings from cohort analyses conducted by others. Furthermore, textbook writers, journalists, policymakers, and others who interpret, summarize, or use the findings of social scientific research increasingly need to understand the principles, potential, and limitations of cohort analysis.

The purpose of this paper is to provide elementary knowledge of cohort analysis and to develop the ability to conduct the simpler forms of analysis with survey sample data. No instruction is given in the demographic techniques of cohort analysis or in the more complicated techniques developed for use with survey sample data, although the latter are briefly described. Detailed treatment of the more complicated techniques is avoided not solely to keep the presentation understandable to readers lacking advanced training in statistics and mathematics; it is avoided also because there are as yet no published examples of fruitful applications of the more complicated techniques and, for reasons discussed below, the assumptions which must be met before those techniques will yield interpretable results are so stringent that the techniques should rarely be used.

BASIC CONCEPTS

The term *cohort* originally referred to a Roman military unit, and a common dictionary definition is still "a group of warriors or soldiers." Now, however, in nontechnical language the term more often than not is used to refer to a person who is one's companion, accomplice, peer, or associate, or in a collective sense, to a band or a group. This usage foreshadows the adaptation of the term into the technical language of demography (which is the study of the size, composition, and distribution of human populations), in which a cohort is defined as those people within a geographically or otherwise delineated population who experienced the same significant life event within a given period of time. Cohort boundaries are arbitrarily delineated, since the "given period of time" may be of any length, from a day (or less) to 20 years (or more), and it may begin at any arbitrarily selected point in time. The cohorts used for social scientific research usually consist of people who experienced a common significant life event within a period of from one to 10 years. The "significant life event" is more often than not birth, in which case the cohort is termed a *birth cohort*. (Unfortunately, the term *age cohort* is sometimes used synonymously with birth cohort, which tends to be confusing, since a birth cohort is not the same as an age level, and kinds of cohorts are most precisely identified by the significant life event which defines them.) However, there are also marriage cohorts, educational cohorts (persons who completed a certain level of education during the same year or other period of time), and cohorts defined by the birth of the first child, by becoming widowed, by retirement, and by divorce. Persons first elected to a legislative body at the same time constitute a kind of cohort, as do persons who entered a graduate program during the same semester or quarter.

Cohort analysis may deal with any kind of cohort, but it usually deals with birth cohorts, and when the word cohort is used without a modifier, the implied modifier is almost always birth, unless the context makes clear that some other meaning is intended.

The term *generation* is sometimes used synonymously with birth cohort, or it may refer to a birth cohort with "natural" rather than arbitrary boundaries. In the latter sense, it consists of a birth cohort (or of adjacent birth cohorts) internally homogeneous in some important respect and distinctly different from persons born earlier or later. For instance, persons whose early formative experiences occurred during the Great Depression may be considered a generation in this sense. Such usage has not promoted clarity of communication, since "generation" has a distinctly different meaning in kinship terminology. Therefore, insofar as possible, such usage of the word should be avoided, but one must be aware of this meaning to understand much of the literature reporting cohort analyses.

Most cohort analysts use the term *cohort analysis* to refer to any study in which there are measures of some characteristic of one or more cohorts (birth or otherwise) at two or more points in time. The term is not ordinarily applied to studies in which different cohorts are compared at one point in time (*cross-sectional* or *synchronic* studies). A few authors do refer to such studies as cohort analyses, and whereas terminological conventions should not be so rigid as to preclude such usage, the term is used here to refer only to studies with a temporal dimension—only to those which are in some respect *diachronic*. Most cohort analyses involve simultaneous synchronic and diachronic comparisons, and therein, according to the proponents of cohort analysis, lies its unique analytic utility.

The simplest of cohort analyses, according to the definition used here, would be a comparison of the characteristics of one cohort at two points in time. For instance, persons born in 1920-1924 might be studied in 1940, when they were 16-20 years old, and in 1945, when they were 21-25 years old. In other words, this would be a study of change in the cohort from one point in time to another, or a simple *intracohort trend study*. Such studies can be useful for some purposes, but the utility is enhanced when there are data for more than one cohort and for more than two points in time.

An intracohort trend study is similar to a *panel study*, the difference being that the same specific individuals are studied at two or more points in time in a panel study, and the total amount of individual change—including changes which offset one another in the aggregate data (summary data on all people studied)—is measured. In an intracohort trend study, in contrast, samples of individuals from the cohort are typically studied, and it is unlikely that any of the individuals studied at time one will also be in the sample at time two. Even when there are data on all surviving members of a cohort, the data are aggregated (are summary data for the entire cohort, or some significant segment of it), so that offsetting individual changes are not measured. For instance, suppose that 20 percent of the members of a cohort were Republican in 1960 and that 20 percent were also Republican in 1970. This lack of net change in percentage Republican does not mean that no movement into and out of the Republican category occurred—only that any movements in the two directions were equal. A panel study will reveal how many individual changes in party identification occurred, but an intracohort trend study will deal only with the net effect of those changes.

Some authors use the adjective *longitudinal* to refer to both intracohort trend studies and panel studies, while some terminological purists apply this adjective only to panel studies. The former usage has the greater utility, since there is no need for a synonym for panel study but there is a need for a term to cover both panel and intracohort trend studies, which have much in common, and to distinguish them from other kinds of diachronic studies, which deal with trends in entire populations, or in segments of populations other than cohorts. The results of longitudinal studies (both panel and intracohort) reflect influences associated with human aging (although, as I point out below, they fail to isolate the effects of aging from the effects of other influences), whereas other diachronic studies do not.

Typically, a cohort analysis involves data on trends in more than one cohort and involves synchronic, or cross-sectional, intercohort comparisons as well. Suppose, for instance, that one has comparable data from national samples of individuals age 20 and older in 1940, 1950, 1960, and 1970. If the exact ages of the persons who responded to the survey are coded, one can construct what I call, for convenience, a *standard cohort table*; that is, a table in which sets of cross-sectional data for the different dates are justaposed and in which the intervals between the points in time for which there are data correspond in years with the intervals used to delineate the birth cohorts. (It will become apparent that such a table has several advantages over any other kind of cohort table, but often the available data do not allow its construction.) In such a table, intercohort comparisons can be made by reading down the columns; intracohort trends can be traced by reading diagonally down and to the right; and trends at each age level as the different cohorts replace one another can be traced by reading across the rows.

The discussion from this point on can be facilitated by examination of a standard cohort table; and sensitivity to the problems encountered by cohort analysts can best be developed by use of real rather than hypothetical data. The data in Table 1 are the percentages of respondents who said they had a "great deal" of interest in politics in response to a question

TABLE 1
Percentage of Respondents Who Reported
a "Great Deal" of Interest in Politics[1], United States

Age	Year		
	1952 (N)	1960 (N)[2]	1968 (N)
21 – 28	19.0 (1,555)	18.4 (447)	18.7 (498)
29 – 36	22.0 (1,756)	22.3 (619)	17.4 (482)
37 – 44	24.1 (1,527)	24.8 (655)	17.0 (501)
45 – 52	28.6 (1,281)	21.7 (498)	20.5 (496)
53 – 60	30.7 (1,035)	28.7 (451)	19.0 (407)
61 – 68	33.8 (779)	27.8 (450)	18.9 (300)
69 – 76	37.3 (431)	30.0 (240)	23.0 (202)
Total	25.7 (8,364)	24.2 (3,360)	18.9 (2,886)

Source: American Institute of Public Opinion (American Gallup) Surveys 502, 503, 504, 636, 757, and 758.

[1]Standardized to a sex ratio or 100. Reported percentages are the means of the male and female percentages.

[2]Weighted N. The number of respondents is about one-half of the reported N.

asked on American Gallup polls in 1952, 1960, and 1968. Eight-year birth cohorts are used to correspond with the eight-year intervals between the dates. Cohorts can be traced through time by reading diagonally down and to the right.

The variation in the percentages in the table can be classified into three kinds of effects (in addition to the effects of sampling error and of compositional changes within aging cohorts) according to the kinds of influences which produce them. Those produced by influences associated with aging are *age effects*, those produced by influences associated with birth cohort membership are *cohort effects*, and those produced by influences associated with each period of time are *period effects*. Unfortunately, there is no straightforward way of identifying these effects through examination or statistical analysis of the cohort table, for at least three basic reasons.

(1) In survey sample data, much of the variation in percentages (or other values) among the cells of a cohort table reflects sampling variability, or the fact that the values in the sample do not correspond precisely with the values in the sampled population. (In the case of the data in Table 1, the population is noninstitutionalized civilians in the United States ages 21 through 76.) Readers familiar with techniques for inferring characteristics of populations from sample data know that one can never be absolutely certain that a given difference or pattern of variation in sample data did not result from sampling error; but probability theory—applied in the form of tests of significance (see Henkel, 1976)—allows estimation of the probability that an observed difference would appear in a randomly drawn sample of a given size if there were no difference in the population. Probability theory can be used to deal with sampling variability in cohort tables, but unfortunately, the specifics of such analysis are not yet well developed. They probably soon will be, as creative statisticians increasingly turn their attention to cohort analysis; nevertheless, a definitive separation of the effects of sampling variability from age, cohort, and period effects will not be possible.

(2) As a birth cohort grows older, it suffers attrition due to the death of some of its members; if those who die differ on the average from those who survive in regard to the phenomenon being studied (the dependent variable), some of the intracohort and cross-sectional variation in the cohort table may reflect this compositional change within cohorts. Or, the compositional change may reduce the variation by offsetting other influences. Similarly, compositional change within cohorts may occur due to migration into and out of the population being studied. The effects of mortality are genuine "age effects," so far as the entire cohort is concerned, but the theoretical interest is almost always with the typical effects of aging on individuals—even when technically the unit of analysis is the cohort rather than the individual. Likewise, migration into and out of the population results in genuine period effects in entire cohorts and in the entire population, but the cohort analyst is usually interested in typical period effects on individuals. Therefore, attempts must usually be made to separate compositional effects from the kinds of age, cohort, and period effects of interest to the analyst. First, to minimize variation in compositional effects due to migration, one should usually limit cohort analyses to relatively "closed" populations, that is, to populations—such as those of most national societies—into which and out of which there is little movement. Then, there are standardization procedures, described below, which can be used for a tentative separation of some of the compositional effects

due to mortality from the other effects in a cohort table. However, the separation can never be definitive, since it is impossible to know precisely how the deceased members of a cohort would have been distributed on a dependent variable at any given time if they had survived.

(3) Regardless of how a cohort table is examined, two of the basic effects (age, cohort, and period) are confounded with one another: age and cohort effects in the cross-sectional data in each column; age and period effects in each cohort diagonal; and cohort and period effects in each row. Readers familiar with research designed to study the effects of such variables as social mobility, status inconsistency, and lack of "status integration" should recognize the confounding of effects in a cohort table as an example of what Blalock (1966; 1967) has called the "identification problem," which occurs when an independent variable in an analysis is a perfect function of two (or more) other variables of theoretical interest (and which, therefore, should also be used as independent variables or as control variables). Stated differently, there is linear dependency of one independent variable on two (or more) other variables which should be controlled or used as independent variables. In the cohort table, age is a perfect function of cohort membership and period of time, cohort membership is a perfect function of age and period, and period is a perfect function of age and cohort membership. For instance, if one knows that a person was 25 years old in 1940, one knows in which of the eight-year cohorts represented in Table 1 the person has membership. Likewise, if one knows the person's cohort membership, one knows in which age range the person was at each date.

Therefore, in a regression analysis—or in any kind of statistical analysis designed to estimate the effects of a number of independent variables on a dependent variable—age, cohort, and period cannot all three be entered as independent variables, although any two can be. However, when two are used as independent variables, the estimate of the effects of each is "contaminated" by the confounding of its effects with those of the third variable (see Uslaner, forthcoming).

This point is so crucial, and has so often not been well understood by cohort analysts, that further elaboration and illustration are in order. Consider the cross-sectional data in the first column of Table 1. The reported interest in politics was generally greater at the older than at the younger age levels. In these data, age and cohort effects are confounded, which means that there are two possible explanations for the variation in reported interest in politics, either or both of which may be correct. The variation could be a function of age, or its close correlates—that is, the older people may have developed a greater average interest in politics as a result of growing older or of progressing through the stages of the life cycle. Or, the older people, as a whole, could have been more interested in politics than the younger people because of their unique formative experiences and "cohort situations." Or, age and cohort influences may both have contributed to the variation. From the data in the column alone, there is no way to choose among these alternative explanations.

Similarly, the confounding of age and period effects is illustrated by the indicated changes in interest in politics from 1960 to 1968 in each cohort for which data for both dates are shown in Table 1. If the indicated intra-cohort change did not result from sampling variability (and it is unlikely to have resulted from sampling variability in all of the cohorts), it could have resulted from aging or progression through the stages of the life cycle, or it could have resulted from general changes in the society from 1960 to 1968. Or, it could have resulted from both age and period influences. In other words, the members of each cohort were subjected not only to stimuli associated with growing older but also to stimuli associated with social and cultural change, and either or both sets of stimuli could have produced the intracohort changes.

The confounding of cohort and period effects is illustrated by the indicated decline in interest in politics from 1952 to 1960 and from 1960 to 1968 at the 69-76 age level (the last row in Table 1). The decline could have resulted from changes in influences associated with each period of time (period influences) or from cohort succession, whereby a cohort with different formative experiences replaced the previous cohort from each date to the next.[1]

Researchers who have been aware of the confounding of age, cohort, and period effects have often believed that the effects could be "unconfounded" through statistical analysis. Even if one recognizes that two kinds of effects are confounded in each column, cohort diagonal, and row of a cohort table—and knows that the effects cannot be separated when each column, diagonal, or row is considered by itself—one may still maintain that by using all or most of the data in the table, each kind of effect can be isolated from the other two. It is true, as we shall see later, that simultaneous use of data for different age levels, cohorts, and periods can provide clues, can provide *tentative* evidence, as to the relative contributions of age, cohort, and period influences to variation in a cohort table. However, it is also true that such procedures cannot provide definitive evidence—that a strictly statistical solution to the age-cohort-period problem is not possible—since identical cohort tables could result from different combinations of age, cohort, and period influences. The cohort table shows effects but gives no direct evidence on the influences which produced those effects.

An illustration with hypothetical data should make the point clearer. The data in Table 2 are the percentages of persons who were "conservatives" at each of five age levels in a hypothetical country in 1940, 1950, 1960, and 1970. The percentages in the first row and column are set more or less arbitrarily; the variation in the first row is assumed to result from a trend away from conservative influences on pre-adult socialization, and the variation in the first column is assumed to result largely from formative influences of the cohorts prior to 1940. The remaining percentages can be derived from those in the first row and column and from the following assumptions concerning age and period influences:

(1) There was a constant level of anticonservative influences (influences for change away from conservatism) in the society during each decade represented in the table, and the magnitude of the influences was such that, in the absence of opposing influences, the percentage of conservatives would have been reduced by 10 points in each cohort during each decade.

(2) Aging exerted no influence toward rigidity, away from suceptibility to change, on the cohort members.

(3) Aging exerted a proconservative influence, but in a nonlinear fashion, so that, in the absence of opposing influences, aging from

TABLE 2
Hypothetical Data on Percentage of Persons Conservative

Age	Year			
	1940	1950	1960	1970
20 – 29	60	50	40	30
30 – 39	62	52	42	32
40 – 49	66	56	46	36
50 – 59	72	62	52	42
60 – 69	80	70	60	50

20-29 to 30-39 would have increased the percentage of conservatives by two points, aging from 30-39 to 40-49 would have increased the percentage by four points, aging from 40-49 to 50-59
would have increased it by six points, and aging from 50-59 to 60-
69 would have increased it by eight points.

However, the percentages in Table 2 can also be derived by beginning with
the same percentages in the first row and column and substituting a different set of assumptions concerning age and period influences:

(1) There were constant influences toward change in an anticonservative direction during each decade represented in the table.

(2) Aging exerted no influence toward change in either a conservative
or an anticonservative direction.

(3) Aging exerted an influence away from susceptibility to change, so
that the constant level of anticonservative stimuli brought about an
eight-point reduction in percentage of conservatives in each cohort
which aged from 20-29 to 30-39 during any decade, a six-point
reduction in any cohort which aged from 30-39 to 40-49, a four-
point reduction in any cohort which aged from 40-49 to 50-59,
and a two-point reduction in any cohort which aged from 50-59 to
60-69 during any one of the decades.[2]

Since the purpose of cohort analysis has often been to estimate whether
or not aspects of the aging process tend to influence people to be more
conservative (see Glenn, 1974), it would be important (if the data were
real rather than hypothetical) to decide whether the effects shown in the
table were likely to have resulted from the first or from the second set of
influences which could have produced them. However, it is obvious that
statistical analysis alone cannot provide a choice between the alternatives.
Therefore, the choice, if it is made, must come from use of theory, evidence from outside the cohort table, and any knowledge one has, from
any source, of the phenomena being investigated.[3]

This discussion leads to a very important principle, which is emphasized
throughout this essay: *Cohort analysis should never be a mechanical exercise uninformed by theory and by evidence from outside the cohort table.*
This principle cannot be stressed too much. Mechanical, atheoretical cohort analyses are, at best, a waste of time, and they are likely to lead to
incorrect conclusions which may become widely accepted and which may
influence policy decisions. It is crucial, therefore, that they be avoided.

Readers with a high need for certitude and a low tolerance for ambig-
uity may at this point be disillusioned with cohort analysis and may be dis-
inclined to read on. If the statistical techniques of cohort analysis cannot
provide definitive evidence as to what causes what, then should not one

search for better techniques of investigation? Indeed, for some purposes for which cohort analysis has been used, better techniques *are* available and should be used instead (although most of them also will not provide definitive evidence of causation). For other purposes, however, cohort analysis is the best available means of investigation, or else it is a valuable supplement to other techniques. Furthermore, in the hands of persons knowledgeable of theories of aging and of recent history, cohort analysis can often lead to reasonable conclusions in which one can have high confidence. The cohort analyst must usually set forth his or her conclusions with a certain amount of tentativeness, but that does not make him unique among social scientific researchers, who are seldom able to arrive at definitive evidence of causation. The person who must have certitude, who cannot embrace conclusions tentatively, should not be engaged in social scientific research.

THE USES OF COHORT ANALYSIS WITH SURVEY SAMPLE DATA

Sensitivity to the kinds of research problems for which cohort analysis is useful and appropriate can best be developed by illustration, and several illustrations are presented later in this paper as various specific techniques are discussed. However, in order to give the reader a good sense of purpose, it is necessary at this point to describe in general terms the most frequent kinds of uses of cohort analysis with survey sample data.

STUDIES OF AGING

The most common purpose of cohort analysis, other than in studies of fertility, has been to investigate the effects of human aging and of its close correlates, the most numerous cohort studies being those designed to estimate the effects of aging on aspects of political attitudes and behavior, such as party identification and voter turnout. (See, for example, Crittenden, 1962, 1963; Cutler, 1968, 1970; Glenn and Grimes, 1968; Glenn and Hefner, 1972; Knoke and Hout, 1974; Hout and Knoke, 1975; and Abramson, 1974, 1975, 1976.) Other studies have dealt with the effects of aging on such variables as tolerance of ideological nonconformity (Culter and Kaufman, 1977), drinking alcoholic beverages (Glenn and Zody, 1970), church attendance (Wingrove and Alston, 1974), political alienation (Cutler and Bengtson, 1974), and mental ability (Baltes and Reinert, 1969; Schaie and Strother, 1968a, 1968b). Cohort studies currently underway are designed to investigate the effects of aging on such diverse phenomena as political knowledge, religious beliefs, sexual permissiveness-restrictiveness, racial and ethnic prejudice, and various dimensions of conservatism-liberalism. In addition, some of the studies are concerned with the effects of aging on susceptibility to attitudinal and behavioral change.

The general strategy in such studies has been to examine intracohort trends and to try, by various means, to decide to what extent the trends reflect influences associated with aging rather than period influences. When the concern has been with the effects of aging on susceptibility to change, measured changes during given periods of time in cohorts at different age levels have been compared (see Glenn and Hefner, 1972; Glenn, 1974; and Cutler and Kaufman, 1975).

The theoretical and practical reasons for investigating the effects of aging have been varied. For instance, some studies have been designed in part to test "disengagement theory" (Cumming and Henry, 1961), or the notion that the person who becomes elderly and other persons in the society tend to mutually terminate their involvement with one another to prepare for the person's death. For instance, the study by Glenn and Grimes (1968) is concerned with whether or not the elderly "disengage" in the sense of withdrawing from political participation and losing interest in politics. Other studies have been concerned with the effects on the potential for social, cultural, and political change of the predicted increase during the next few decades in the median age of the population of the United States and of most other societies.

The meaning of the phrase "effects of aging" differs according to the purpose of the study, since human aging consists of a large number of imperfectly correlated dimensions. In its most elemental sense, aging is merely the passage of time after birth (chronological aging), and it is only this dimension of aging with which cohort analysis can directly deal. However, influences on attitudes and behavior are rarely attributed to chronological aging per se; rather, they are attributed to dimensions of biological, psychological, and social aging—all of which are rather close, although imperfect, correlates of chronological aging.

Biological aging consists of a predictable sequence of physiological changes which occur along with chronological aging. Although the sequence of changes in any one aspect of the body is invariant (or almost so) among individuals and populations, the rate of biological aging varies among individuals, presumably for both environmental and hereditary reasons. Social aging is the characteristic sequence of changes in the status, roles, and relationships to other persons which the individual experiences along with chronological aging. Social aging is similar to biological aging in that its rate varies among individuals, but it differs in that its sequence of changes differs substantially among societies and subcultures, and even some individuals within a subculture do not go through the typical sequence of changes. Psychological aging consists of the characteristic sequence of changes in personality—including attitudes, values, and behavioral tendences—associated with chronological aging. Since psychological aging is presumably a consequence of both biological and social aging, its rate is variable among individuals, and its sequence of changes is variable among both societies and individuals, but less variable than that of social aging.

Each of the major aspects of aging consists, in turn, of several imperfectly correlated dimensions. That is, each stage of each kind of aging consists of several changes which characteristically occur together but do not always do so. For instance, different parts and aspects of the body may age at different rates, as when a prematurely gray-haired person retains the vigor characteristic of young adulthood. Or, with respect to social aging, a man may first become a father in his fifties, shortly before his retirement, thus combining a "young adult" role with roles characteristic of late middle age.

All cohort studies designed to study the effects of any one, or any combination, of the many dimensions of aging have used chronological aging as the indicator. Conceivably, a study might be designed which would measure the characteristics of surviving cohort members at specified stages on some dimension of biological, social, or psychological aging rather than at specified intervals of time. However, such a study would be extremely difficult and expensive, and as we shall see below, cohort analysts usually must rely on data collected by other researchers for purposes other than cohort analysis. Therefore, it is improbable that many cohort analyses will ever be conducted which do not use chronological aging as the indicator of the relevant dimension or dimensions of aging.

Although the use of such an indirect indicator of the independent variable of interest may entail marked errors in the case of a few individuals, it is unlikely to introduce much error into summary measures for an entire birth cohort (or any other kind of cohort), since different individual errors tend to offset one another. Nevertheless, the necessity to use chronological aging as an indicator of all dimensions of aging does create a problem, because it confounds the effects of the different dimensions. Therefore, an empirical separation of the effects of the different dimensions of aging is not possible through cohort analysis alone. For this as well as several other reasons, it is often desirable to supplement cohort analyses with other techniques appropriate for investigating the effects of aging.

Three other methods to study the effects of aging are commonly used, and it is important for cohort analysts to be familiar with each in order to decide whether or not one or more of them should be used instead of, or in addition to, cohort analysis. These methods are *cross-sectional, panel,* and *retrospective* studies. The first two are discussed briefly above, but additional discussion is needed.

Cross-sectional studies designed to study the effects of aging compare, for the same period of time, persons at different stages of aging. (Although data for several points in time may be utilized, each comparison involves only one time period.) Cross-sectional and cohort studies are not completely distinct, of course, since a cohort study usually includes a number of cross-sectional comparisons, but a strictly cross-sectional study does not involve examination of intracohort trends or trends at each age level. Furthermore, cross-sectional studies usually entail analyses over and above those which can be performed with data from the usual kind of cohort table. For instance, cross-sectional comparisons may utilize measures of biological, social, or psychological age instead of, or in addition to, chronological age, so that the effects of different dimensions of aging can be at least tentatively separated from one another. Studies have compared persons of the same (or similar) chronological age who were at different stages of the life cycle (social age)—retired persons versus those not retired; parents with children still at home versus parents whose children have left home (Glenn, 1975a); and so forth. In addition, some variables can easily be controlled in a strictly cross-sectional study which cannot very easily be controlled in a cohort study—for reasons detailed below.

It should be apparent, therefore, that, contrary to widespread belief, cohort studies are not in all respects superior to cross-sectional studies for the purpose of detecting effects of aging. In fact, the cohort analyst who is a careful and thorough researcher will usually do a number of cross-sectional analyses in addition to those which can be conducted with data from the cohort table. Furthermore, when data appropriate for cohort analysis are not available, a cross-sectional research design can often yield evidence almost as nearly definitive as that which could be derived from a cohort study.

As I point out above, a panel study traces the characteristics of specific individuals through time. Panel studies share with intracohort trend studies the confounding of age and period effects, and they usually provide fewer clues than a cohort study to help unconfound those effects. In some panel studies not designed to study the effects of aging, very nearly definitive evidence of causation can be derived because a "tight" experimental design can be used or approximated. That is, a stimulus can be administered to an experimental group but withheld from a control group closely matched on a number of relevant characteristics. It is obvious, however that most of the stimuli associated with aging cannot be withheld from a control group, and hence an experimental design cannot be approximated in panel studies designed to study age effects, and it is not possible to separate definitively the effects of aging from the effects of other stimuli which impinge on panel members during the study.

Panel studies do have some advantages over cohort studies, however. As noted above, panel studies allow detection of offsetting changes among different cohort members, and more important, they allow use of measures of biological, social, and psychological aging. They would often be valuable supplements to cohort studies, but any panel study to detect the effects of aging must be conducted over a period of years and involves an enormous expenditure of time and money relative to the increment in evidence typically gained. It is unlikely, therefore, that many readers of this paper who conduct cohort studies will be willing and able to supplement their cohort data with panel data.

An additional kind of study valuable for aging research involves retrospective reports, that is, information from respondents on their recollections of their behavior, attitudes, and affective states at some earlier point (or points) in time. Of course, recall may be inaccurate, and even if respondents accurately report how they have changed, the reported changes reflect both period influences and influences associated with aging. That is, retrospective trend data share with panel and intracohort trend data a confounding of age and period effects. However, respondents may have insights into why they have changed, or at least their explanations can usefully be taken into account. For instance, a person who has changed his political orientation may attribute that change to a number of important national events, or perhaps to an aspect of social aging, such as marriage and the assumption of family responsibilities.

Obviously, a retrospective study would almost always be a useful adjunct to a cohort study, but if the researcher does not have the resources to gather his or her own data and must rely on available data, combining retrospective and cohort studies is rarely possible.

Studies of Social and Cultural Change

In an influential essay published more than a decade ago, Norman Ryder (1965) argues convincingly for the utility of the cohort as a unit for the study of social and cultural change. However, Ryder's essay does not deal with specific techniques of research, and although it has been very frequently cited, it has led to few attempts to use cohort analysis for the primary purpose of studying change. Furthermore, the few attempts to follow Ryder's recommendations, including one by this author (Glenn, 1972), suffer from inadequately developed and refined techniques of analysis. Therefore, a discussion of cohort analysis for the study of change must deal primarily with potential rather than with techniques of demonstrated utility.

It is obvious that social and cultural change from time one to time two in a society experiencing little emigration or immigration will occur primarily through

(1) changes in the characteristics of, and interrelations among, individuals who are in the population of the society at both times one and two, and

(2) cohort succession, or the entry of new individuals into the society through birth and the exit of other individuals through death. (If the concern is with the adult population only, entry will be through aging rather than birth.)

To the extent that cohorts entering the population differ from those whose members are rapidly dying, the flow of birth cohorts through the population will transform the aggregate characteristics of the population. If the entering and exiting cohorts differ little from one another, the short-term changes wrought by cohort succession will be minuscule; and even if the cohorts differ substantially, the change will not be very rapid. In modern societies, in which birth and death rates are both characteristically low, people in the population at time one will remain a majority of the population at almost any later time for which the cohort analyst is likely to have data. In these societies, social and cultural change through cohort succession is necessarily gradual.

Furthermore, some differences between entering and exiting cohorts will bring about little or no change in the population, since the effects of the differences will be almost precisely offset by changes among individuals who are in the population at both times one and two. For instance, suppose that, as conventional wisdom would have it, cohorts entering adulthood tend to be liberal, that the individuals in them tend to become more conservative as they grow older, and that older cohorts experiencing heavy mortality are predominantly conservative. In such a case, if the currently entering cohorts are not more liberal than were the currently exiting cohorts when the latter entered adulthood, cohort succession will cause no change in liberalism-conservatism except that caused by any change in age distribution due to differences in the numbers of individuals in the different cohorts. Therefore, cohort succession will ordinarily lead to an important degree of social and cultural change only when the entering and exiting cohorts differ in their relatively permanent characteristics—when the differences are not solely the result of differences in age and stage of the life cycle. In other words, cohort succession will lead to change over and above that associated with changes in the age distribution only if the differences between entering and exiting cohorts are "cohort effects" rather than "age effects."

As I stress earlier in this paper, a definitive separation of cohort effects from age effects is not possible from an analysis of the cohort data alone. In a comparison of entering and exiting cohorts, the cohort data will not even provide many clues for such a separation, since the time span covered by most of the series of data currently available for cohort analysis almost never allows comparisons of entering and exiting cohorts when they were young adults or were at any other age level. Nevertheless, if, as is often the case, theory or evidence of any kind suggests that aging has little effect on the dependent variable of interest, it may be useful to estimate how much of the total change in the population between two points in time resulted from cohort succession (Glenn, 1972). It may be of theoretical interest or practical utility to know the approximate relative importance in bringing about observed change of

(1) differences in the socialization and early formative experiences of the cohorts, and
(2) influences affecting people of all ages and in all cohorts.

In addition, cohort data can be brought to bear on important theoretical and practical questions relating to social and cultural change without there being any attempt to assess the amount of change due to cohort succession. For instance, there is value simply in comparing the amount of change between time one and time two in older and younger cohorts, since there are theoretical reasons for expecting greater change in the younger cohorts. For a variety of reasons (discussed in detail later), persons aging beyond young adulthood are likely to become less susceptible to change in at least some kinds of values, attitudes, and behavior—both because they are likely to become somewhat insulated against exposure to the stimuli which prompt change and because they are likely to become less responsive to the stimuli to which they are exposed. Some evidence supports this notion that aging cohorts become less prone to change (see Culter and Kaufman, 1973; and Glenn, 1974), but the magnitude and pervasiveness (in terms of kinds of attitudes involved) of any "rigidity effect" wrought by aging has not been established.

More nearly definitive evidence on this issue would be useful not only to theorists who would understand social, cultural, and political change but also to social planners and activists who would promote (or oppose) change. For instance, persons directing campaigns to change attitudes and behavior who "write off" older persons as a "lost cause" are making a serious strategic error if in fact many older persons are amenable to many kinds of change.

DATA SOURCES

Few researchers are likely to conduct cohort analyses exclusively with data from surveys which they themselves have designed or which anyone has designed expressly for the study being undertaken. In other words, cohort analyses with survey sample data are usually "secondary analyses" (see Hyman, 1972), that is, they utilize available data originally collected for some other purpose. In order for a researcher to collect his or her own data for a cohort analysis, he or she would have to devote some time to the study over a period of at least as many years as the span of time covered by the analysis, and the better cohort studies usually cover a span of 20 or more years. Few researchers are likely to be willing to devote time to designing a study which will yield publishable results only in the distant future, and it would be difficult to get funding for such a project. Therefore, cohort analysis must usually be restricted to dependent variables on which for some reason data have been gathered periodically from national samples over a period of years. Obviously, the would-be cohort analyst must know what appropriate data are available before he or she plans the research.

Most, although by no means all, of the American national survey data appropriate for cohort analysis are available from two major survey data archives: the Roper Public Opinion Research Center in Williamstown, Massachusetts, and the Survey data Archive of the Institute for Social Research at the University of Michigan, Ann Arbor. Data sets may be borrowed or purchased from these two archives by any academic researcher (and in many cases, by non-academic researchers as well), but use of the data is greatly facilitated if one's college or university has membership in the two inter-university organizations formed to provide access to the archives. Access to the Roper Center data is provided by the International Survey Library Association (ISLA), in which about 50 colleges and universities (mostly in the United States) are members. Faculty members and students at member institutions are entitled to use of the data at no cost to themselves up to a certain level for each institution each year. Frequency distributions and cross-tabulations may be ordered from the Center, or entire data sets may be bought (or borrowed, in the case of some sets) on punch cards or magnetic tape. Access to the data in the Survey Research Archive of the Michigan Institute for Social Research is provided by the Inter-University Consortium for Political and Social Research (ICPSR), in which more than 200 colleges and universities are members. A member institution can request any data set in the archive, and most data sets can be provided either on cards or on tape. The codebooks for a large number of the data sets (those classified as Type I) are routinely sent to the member institutions, and other codebooks are available on request. (The membership fee does not cover the cost of tapes or of duplicate codebooks.)

Space limitations preclude a listing here of even the most important of the questions repeated on U.S. national surveys several times over a period of years for which data are available from the Roper Center or the ISR Archive. However, two reference works are available (or soon will be) which will enable the researcher quickly to identify many of the series of questions appropriate for cohort analysis.

The first is a volume published in 1975 by the Roper Center and the Social Science Research Council entitled *Survey Data for Trend Analysis: An Index of Repeated Questions in U.S. National Surveys Held by the Roper Public Opinion Research Center.* The index lists all questions on surveys held by the Center which were repeated with identical, or almost identical, wording at an interval of at least a year (between the first and last asking) between September 1936 and October 1973. Some of the questions will be of little or no interest to cohort analysts, since they deal with issues of ephemeral interest, but the 451-page listing includes many questions likely to be of interest to almost any cohort analyst.

The second major reference tool, which is being prepared as this paper is being written, will be a compilation of data from questions repeated on the Michigan Survey Research Center National Election Studies from 1952 through 1974. The age categories used for reporting the data will allow simple cohort studies without further analysis, and the data sets for the Election Studies are available from the ISR Survey Data Archive. Readers who are students of American government and politics will already be familiar with the Election Studies, which have been conducted every two years since 1948, except in 1950. The 1948, 1954, and 1962 studies are modest surveys of limited scope, but the other Election Studies provide a series of repeated questions on a variety of political variables, including, of course, party identification and voter turnout. Among the variables covered by several of the surveys are trust in people, trust in government, media exposure, political knowledge, interest in public affairs, approval of protest activities, and judgements of the most important social problem in the country.

Prominent among the data at the Roper Center which are appropriate for cohort analysis are those collected by the pioneer commercial opinion polling organization, the American Institute of Public Opinion (the Gallup Poll). In spite of some difficulties (discussed later) in using the early Gallup data, they are an especially rich resource for cohort analysts; some of the Gallup series of questions, along with exact age codes, extend back to 1937.[4] Since Gallup has often conducted a national survey about every three weeks, some questions have been repeated dozens of times, and often data from polls conducted within a short period of time can be pooled to form the large sample sizes for age levels which are needed for cohort analysis. Undoubtedly, the Gallup data constitute the most valuable single data resource available to cohort analysts, although so far they have been used for very few cohort studies.

In addition to the Roper-Center-SSRC index described above, sources of information about the Gallup data include a three-volume compilation of Gallup data entitled *The Gallup Poll*; a monthly periodical entitled *The Gallup Opinion Index,* published since 1966, which reports current Gallup data and occasionally trend data from earlier polls; and "The Polls" section which appeared in each issue of *The Public Opinion Quarterly* from 1961 until the death of the compiler, Hazel Erskine, in 1975.

Other American survey data appropriate for cohort analysis are held by the National Opinion Research Center in Chicago, the Louis Harris polling organization in New York, the Bureau of the Census in Washington, and several relatively small academic data archives, such as the Data Library at the Survey Research Center at the University of California at Berkeley. Unfortunately, there are, to my knowledge, no good indexes to the repeated questions on data sets available from these sources. However, some of the more valuable of the series of repeated questions can be discovered by examining the "Previous Usage" appendix of the codebooks for the General Social Surveys conducted by the National Opinion Research Center in 1972, 1973, 1974, 1975, and 1976. Since the General Social Surveys were designed primarily to extend time series and to provide trend data from established baselines, most of their questions were asked on one or more earlier American national surveys. The "Previous Usage" appendix identifies the earlier surveys and gives the location of their data. Of course, the General Social Surveys themselves, whose data are available from both the Roper Center and the ISR Survey Data Archive, are a very valuable resource to cohort analysts.

The Roper Center has survey data from at least 67 countries in addition to the United States, and the ISR Survey Data Archive has data from several other (mainly Western European) countries. These data sets contain many series of repeated questions appropriate for cohort analysis—a few comparable to series available for the United States. Furthermore, major data archives in several other countries contain good collections of national survey data for those countries—a prominent example being the archive at the University of Essex in the United Kingdom. Comparative studies of aging and of social change with cohort data are either rare or nonexistent (depending on how narrowly one construes the meaning of "comparative study");[5] hence, there are ample opportunities for pioneering research in that realm.

Unfortunately, discovering good series of repeated questions is more difficult for other countries than for the United States (at least for U.S. researchers). The series available from the ISR Survey Data Archive can perhaps best be discovered by direct examination of the codebooks, many of which should be available from the official representative of the ICPSR at each member institution. Discovering appropriate non-American data at the Roper Center or at archives in other countries may require extensive correspondence with the archives and payment for searches of their files.

PROBLEMS OF COMPARABILITY

After researchers have identified a series of repeated questions ostensibly appropriate for cohort analysis, they may find, after examining the codebooks, that the data gathered at different times are not comparable, or are not comparable without recoding, collapsing of response alternatives, or exclusion of some respondents, Or, even when the question wording, response alternatives, and coding are identical, they may discover that differences in sample design prevent the data from the different surveys from being strictly comparable. To complicate matters further, incomparability may result from changes in the meaning of words or phrases or from changes in response bias; or data gathered at two points in time may be incomparable because they were gathered during different phases of a cyclical pattern of change. Most problems of comparability encountered by cohort analysts are not insurmountable, and I do not wish to discourage would-be cohort analysts by making the problems appear more formidable than they are. However, I must discuss them at some length, since a cohort analyst lacking sensitivity to the problems is likely to make serious blunders.

One of the more common reasons for incomparability of ostensibly comparable repeated questions is that on some surveys, but not on others, the question is preceded by a "filter," that is, the question is asked only of those respondents who chose one (or certain) of the response alternatives of a previous question. For instance, questions on school desegregation have sometimes been asked of all respondents and sometimes only of parents of school age children. Of course, responses to filtered and unfiltered questions are not comparable and should not be used in the same cohort study. However, if the "filter" question (such as the presence or absence of school age children) is included on the surveys with the unfiltered version of the question, the kind of respondents who were filtered out on some of the surveys can be excluded from the samples of the other surveys to make the data from the different surveys comparable. Even so, use of a filter on some of the surveys may preclude use of the question for cohort analysis, given the need for a relatively "closed" population, into which and out of which there is little movement. For instance, parents with school age children are not an appropriate population for cohort analysis. In contrast, questions which filter out nonwhites may be used, and even such populations as Catholics and Protestants are probably sufficiently "closed" so that cohort analyses with samples drawn exclusively from one of them will not be seriously affected by movement of individuals into and out of the population.

Another common cause for incomparability which may not be discovered from examining the reference works cited above is the use of different response alternatives even though the wording of the "stem" of the question is identical. Respondents to different surveys may be asked to choose among different lists of response alternatives, or even when the alternatives are identical, the responses may not be coded the same for all surveys. Furthermore, when the wording of the question stem varies slightly, the data may or may not be roughly comparable, depending partly on what response alternatives were used and how the responses were coded. Therefore, final judgements on the comparability of data from series of repeated questions can usually be made only after the codebooks have been carefully examined. Some illustrations should sensitize the reader to some of the kinds of problems likely to be encountered and suggest ways to deal with the problems.

Since the early 1940s, the U.S. Gallup Poll has periodically asked respondents whether or not they knew the name of their congressman. The question wording in the 1940s and 1950s was not identical to that in the 1960s and 1970s, but it seems that the two questions should have elicited the same information since they both asked for a "yes" or a "no" response. However, respondents to the earlier question who said "yes" were asked to name their congressman, and the codes separate the bluffers and the mistaken respondents from those who gave the correct name of their congressman. In contrast, all of the "yes" responses to the later question are lumped together.

In this case, comparability (but not a precise measure of changes in knowledge) can be achieved by recombining into one category the "yes" responses to the earlier question; and on many occasions, collapsing coding categories will provide comparability. If, however, the responses alternatives presented to the respondents, and not just the coding categories, were different, collapsing to achieve comparability should be done with great caution. For instance, in a Gallup series of questions on personal happiness, the following two wordings (among others) were used:

(1) In general, how happy would you say you are—very happy, fairly happy, or not very happy?

(2) In general, how happy would you say you are—very happy, fairly happy, or not at all happy?

When the first version was used, a fourth alternative, "not at all happy," was coded, apparently because some respondents gave that response even though it was not presented to them. Since the problem is partly to make a three-point scale comparable with a four-point scale, and since the labels for the two highest points are the same for both scales, one might think that comparability would result from collapsing the two lower categories of the four-point scale. However, comparability is not so easily achieved, since comparison of responses to the two questions asked at brief intervals reveals that the "fairly happy" alternative was more often chosen when the second version was used. Apparently, some of the "not very happy" persons preferred to say that they were "fairly happy" rather than "not at all happy." Nor should one just assume that the percentages of respondents who said they were "very happy" are comparable, although they apparently are, since they do not vary consistently between the two versions:

	Males	Females	Both Sexes
AIPO 369, April 1946 (version 1)	38.4%	40.1%	39.2%
AIPO 399, June 1947 (version 2)	38.2	38.7	38.0
AIPO 410T, December 1947 (version 1)	37.6	38.0	37.8

Although the two versions of the Gallup "happiness" question can be made comparable by dichotomizing the responses into "very happy" and "all other," neither Gallup version can be made comparable with the happiness question used on surveys conducted by National Opinion Research Center and the Survey Research Center at the University of Michigan, to which the first response alternative is also "very happy." The latter question is:

> Taken all together, how would you say things are these days—would you say that you are very happy, pretty happy, or not too happy?

Comparison of responses to the Gallup and the NORC-SRC questions asked at brief intervals reveals that the Gallup question elicits a somewhat larger percentage of "very happy" responses, apparently because "pretty happy" means to many people a higher degree of happiness than "fairly happy" and thus draws a larger percentage of the responses from the happier people.

In some cases, response categories can be collapsed to attain comparability, but doing so will not yield data very useful for cohort analysis since the collapsed (but not the uncollapsed) data show little or no variation by age. For instance, Gallup has asked a series of job satisfaction questions to which the response alternatives are "satisfied" and "dissatisfied," and the NORC General Social Surveys used the same question stem but asked the respondents to rate themselves as very satisfied, moderately satisfied, a little dissatisfied, or very dissatisfied. Comparing the collapsed responses from the 1973 General Social Survey, conducted in March, with the responses to the job satisfaction question on AIPO 863, conducted in late January of 1973, reveals that the responses to the two versions of the question can be made comparable, or approximately so. However, the NORC surveys consistently show older workers to be somewhat better satisfied as a whole than younger workers (Glenn, Taylor, and Weaver, 1977, forthcoming), most of the variation being within the broad categories of satisfied and dissatisfied workers. Therefore, collapsing the responses removes virtually all of the variation by age and leaves the data of little value to the cohort analyst. This may be an extreme and unusual case, but it is likely that collapsing response categories will often conceal important information from the cohort analyst, in which cases a cross-sectional research design with the uncollapsed data should be chosen as a supplement or an alternative to a cohort design.

The cohort analyst should exercise special care when dealing with a variable which is known to be, or which seems likely to be, subject to considerable short-term fluctuation. An example is church attendance, which varies seasonally and from week to week according to such influences as the weather and the attraction of competing activities. The precise variance of the short-term fluctuation is not known (but might be investigated with available data), but it may be as great as, or greater than, the sampling variance (discussed below). Since the researcher would not ordinarily be interested in attendance during any given week but rather would use the data for that week as an indicator of attendance over a longer period of time, the short-term fluctuation in effect increases the error variance (discussed below) and diminishes the confidence which can be placed in the difference between the attendance levels shown by two surveys. Therefore, any trend study on church attendance should use data from at least three or four surveys from each broad period of interest (for example, the early 1950s or the late 1960s), and the surveys from the different periods should, if possible, be at least crudely matched as to season.

Some variables are likely to rise and fall in response to evenly spaced events such as elections or in response to unevenly spaced phenomena such as economic recessions. For instance, knowledge of the names of congressmen is likely to be greater shortly before and after the congressional elections than at other times, and reported political interest may tend to increase with the approach of a presidential election. (The spacing of the SRC Election Studies prevents incomparability due to cyclical change, but one must be cautious about such possible incomparability when using data on political variables from the opinion polls.) And reports of happiness and other measures of "psychological well-being" are likely to fluctuate with changes in economic conditions. Cohort studies often cannot be based solely on data gathered at comparable phases of the business cycle or at points with equal proximity to elections, but cohort analysts should be sensitive to the possibility that the appearance of long-term intracohort or intercohort trends may result from use of data gathered at different phases of a cyclical pattern of change.

For several reasons, the responses given to survey interviewers (or to written questionnaires) are often inaccurate—sometimes inadvertently and sometimes deliberately so. Such inaccuracies (except for those which are random and thus tend to offset one another in aggregate data) are known as *response bias*. They may result from a desire of the person being interviewed to impress or gain the approval of the interviewer (the *social desirability set*), from a predisposition to choose the positive alternative when a positive and negative response alternative are offered (the *acquiescence set*), or from a variety of other sources (see Sudman and Bradburn, 1974).[6] Any researcher who utilizes survey data should consider how response bias may have affected the data, and the cohort analyst is no exception. Furthermore, in addition to the usual considerations of response bias, the cohort or trend analyst must also consider how changes in response bias may have affected the data.

For instance, it is known that in the recent past, blacks have tended to give different responses to some questions depending on whether the interviewer was white or black (Williams, 1964; 1968). Presumably, the responses given to black interviewers were usually the more accurate and the responses to white interviewers tended to be biased. The interviewers for the early U.S. surveys (at least through the early 1960s) were almost all white, but in recent years such survey organizations as the National Opinion Research Center have striven toward (but have not completely achieved) a racial matching of interviewers and households. This change in the typical race of the interviewers of black respondents may have caused some apparent changes in the attitudes and behavior of blacks which do not reflect real changes, or conversely, changes in interviewer effects may have masked real changes. Furthermore, since bias in the responses of blacks to white interviewers presumably reflected the traditional compliant stance of blacks vis-à-vis whites, racial interviewer effects may have changed in nature and magnitude in recent years.

Available evidence generally indicates that survey respondents tend to "overreport" socially approved behavior and attitudes and to "underreport" disapproved behavior and attitudes. Although the evidence is not definitive in each case, one might expect an overreporting of such phenomena as voting, church attendance, and marital satisfaction and an underreporting of religious agnosticism, violations of the law, illicit sex behavior, and the like. To the extent that approval or disapproval of a kind of behavior or attitude changes, inaccuracy in reports of that phenomenon are likely to change. Therefore, changes in the reported frequency of a kind of behavior in an aging cohort may reflect both changes in the behavior and changes in the norms pertaining to the behavior. For most research purposes, the confounding of these two kinds of effects (either or both of which may be either age or period effects) will pose no serious problems, but when such confounding seems likely, it should be taken into account in interpreting the data.

The meanings survey respondents typically attach to some words and phrases may change through time or may vary by age at any one time. For instance, the typical meanings attached to the terms "liberal" and "conservative" by people in the United States have undoubtedly changed moderately, if not substantially, since opinion pollsters began asking respondents to identify themselves as liberals or conservatives almost 40 years ago. Therefore, a cohort analysis of liberal-conservative identifications would be difficult to interpret and would be of rather limited value at best. Of even less value would be a cohort analysis of "class identification" or so-called "subjective social class," data on which have been gathered by the SRC Election Studies, the General Social Surveys, and a number of U.S. national opinion polls. For instance, respondents to the 1974 General Social Survey were asked:

> If you were asked to use one of four names for your social class, which would you say you belong in: the lower class, the working class, the middle class, or the upper class?

In view of the fact that social scientists cannot agree on the meaning of "social class" or of any of the class labels used in the question, it seems strange that they would expect respondents to social surveys to agree on the meaning. Yet if respondents do not generally agree, the meaning of the responses to the question is ambiguous. Therefore, the value of responses to such a question for any purpose is problematic, and it is especially problematic for cohort studies, since the meanings attached to class labels are likely to vary systematically through time and by age.

It should hardly be necessary to point out that the referent of such terms as "the present administration" and "the government in Washington" changes through time. Such variation may or may not preclude cohort studies with questions containing the terms, depending on the purpose of the research, but usually it will. For instance, in a study designed to study the effects of aging on conservatism, a cohort analysis involving attitudes toward different federal administrations with different positions on the various liberal-conservative continua would not be very useful (and might yield highly misleading results) unless it were used in an unusual and ingenious way. Such usage is best avoided by the novice cohort analyst.

Cohort analyses restricted to data from the SRC Election Studies and other recent national surveys conducted by academic survey organizations will not ordinarily involve any serious problems of comparability due to differences in sample design.[7] However, many cohort analysts will want to use the commercial poll data, since they

(1) provide a greater number of series of repeated questions,

(2) often provide data covering a greater time span, and

(3) often allow pooling of data from several surveys conducted within a short period of time to achieve the large sample sizes needed for cohort analysis.

Unfortunately, however, use of the earlier and later poll data (or later academic survey data) in the same analysis often poses some rather obdurate problems of comparability due to differences in sample design.

Until the early 1950s, all of the commercial polling organizations, as well as some nonprofit survey organizations such as the National Opinion Research Center, drew their samples by the "quota control" method (see Stephan and McCarthy, 1958: 37-38). All "quota" samples are not alike, but they have in common the fact that they contain predetermined proportions of people from certain segments of the population. For instance, it may be determined that individuals in the sample will be distributed by sex, age, region, and size of community in the same manner that the entire adult population was distributed according to the most recent decennial census. Or, if several years have elapsed since the census, estimates (usually extrapolations from census data) of the distribution of the adult population on the quota control variables may be used. Assuming that the estimates are accurate, or nearly so, a quota sample designed to represent the total population is necessarily representative with respect to each of the variables selected for quota controls. Unfortunately, however, some early national quota samples may have been distinctly unrepresentative with respect to variables not subject to the controls. For instance, when such "status" variables as occupation and amount of formal education were not precisely controlled by the quotas, persons in the lower social levels were almost always underrepresented. Such systematic bias was introduced primarily in the final stage of the sampling process, in which interviewers strategically located across the country selected respondents to be interviewed. Each interviewer was assigned a quota of persons with specified characteristics (for example, a certain number of males or a certain number of whites) to interview. Within the limits of the quota, the interviewer had complete discretion in the selection of respondents, and it was primarily this discretion which biased the samples. Understandably, the interviewers tended to select the more accessible of the potential respondents, who may have differed systematically from the less accessible, rarely-at-home persons in many of the attitudes (and other characteristics) studied by the surveys. Apparently, there was a tendency for the interviewers to prefer to work in the safer and more pleasant neighborhoods, which largely accounted for the underrepresentation of low-status persons.

Many of the samples drawn by the polling organizations in the 1930s and 1940s were deliberately designed to underrepresent certain segments of the adult population. For instance, since the earlier Gallup polls were used primarily to predict the outcome of elections and to provide readings on the sentiment of the electorate between elections, the samples were designed to represent each population segment in proportion to the votes it usually cast in elections rather than in proportion to the number of individuals in it. Since voter turnout was relatively low among females, southerners, blacks, and persons with little education, those segments of the population were deliberately underrepresented, and there were no southern blacks in many of the earlier samples.

The most important changes to occur in the Gallup samples were those designed to make them represent the entire adult (age 21 and older) noninstitutionalized population rather than voters only. To complicate matters, these changes did not occur at once but were distributed over a period of almost a decade. For instance, the first Gallup omnibus (general purpose) survey to use a sample with proportional representation of females apparently was AIPO 335, conducted in November of 1944, whereas the first omnibus survey to use a sample with proportional representation of southerners apparently was AIPO 513, conducted in March and April of 1953.

By the mid-1950s, all of the major survey organizations were designing their usual samples to represent the total noninstitutionalized civilian population and had changed from quota control to probability or "modified probability" samples (described below). However, even in the late 1950s and 1960s, low-status persons were not adequately represented in some national samples, at least at some age levels. A result, illustrated by the data in Table 3, is an apparent decrease in the aggregate educational attainments within any birth cohort traced with American Gallup data from the 1940s into the 1960s. Of course, educational attainments did not really decrease within the cohorts but rather increased slightly as some cohort members completed more years of school and as the less educated members suffered higher mortality (partly because they were slightly older on the average). The decrease shown by the data was apparently due largely to a progressively more nearly proportional representation of low-education persons in the Gallup samples, but it may have resulted partly from a persistent underrepresentation of young low-status persons (especially males).

Given this artifactual decrease in education within birth cohorts traced with Gallup data from the 1940s into the 1960s, the data would show a decrease in any dependent variable highly correlated with education even if the level of that variable did not really decrease in the cohort. A similar false appearance of change (or masking or real change) might occur in the case of variables highly correlated with sex, race, or region in birth cohorts traced with Gallup data from the early 1940s to the mid-1950s or later.

Fortunately, most dependent variables of interest to cohort analysts will not be so highly correlated with education, sex, race, or region that changes in sample design will lead to serious distortions in cohort analyses with uncorrected Gallup data. However, there is risk of serious distortion with a few variables, and thus it is wise to perform some simple adjustments (corrections) on cohort data from early Gallup samples to minimize

TABLE 3

Years of School Completed by a 10-Year Cohort of White Males,
as Shown by American Gallup Samples, 1945 through 1965

Years of School Completed	Year: (Age):	1945 (50-59)	1949 (54-63)	1953 (58-67)	1957 (62-71)	1961 (66-71)	1965 (70-79)
0 - 8		43.5	51.0	50.3	57.5	60.9	65.1
1-3 of High School		18.7	15.6	21.0	19.2	15.2	7.9
4 of High School		16.0	16.3	16.1	15.9	15.7	16.7
At Least Some College		21.9	17.1	12.6	7.4	8.2	10.2
Total		100.0	100.0	100.0	100.0	100.0	100.0
(N)		(771)	(812)	(366)	(365)	(440)[1]	(430)[1]

Source: American Institute of Public Opinion (American Gallup) Surveys 353, 360, 364, 377, 432, 433, 434, 435, 521, 522, 523, 524, 578, 580, 582, 587, 639, 647, 649, 702, 706, 709, and 712. Adapted from Glenn and Zody (1970).
[1]Weighted N. The number of respondents is about one-half of the reported N.

the risk. If the adjustments make little difference, then the uncorrected data may be used.

Even when there is no reason to suspect bias due to changes in sample design, it is wise initially to perform cohort analyses separately for males and females. Intracohort change (and other variation shown by cohort data) may vary by sex, and as a cohort grows older, the proportion of females in it becomes greater due to higher mortality among males. To correct for this compositional change in aging cohorts, the male and female data should be kept separate and interpreted separately, or else the data in each cohort at each point in time should be standardized to a sex ratio of 100 (equal proportions of males and females). Such standardization is accomplished simply by computing the mean of the male and female values for each cell in the cohort table. This procedure will simultaneously correct for underrepresentation of females in the early Gallup samples. Since blacks (and other nonwhites) are still a small proportion of the total population, and since the responses of nonwhites to most survey questions have not differed substantially from those of whites, underrepresentation of nonwhites in the early Gallup samples will usually have a negligible effect on cohort data. However, if correction is deemed necessary, it must be accomplished simply by excluding nonwhites from the data for all points in time. Standardization procedures to correct for the underrepresentation of nonwhites are not effective, since nonwhites were too few in many of the early samples to provide reliable estimates of nonwhite attitudes and behavior.

The sources of bias in the early Gallup samples most likely to distort cohort data are the underrepresentation of southerners and low-education people; even so, it is rare that corrections for such bias will substantially alter the data. Furthermore, adjustment for either source of bias is, by itself, easily accomplished. Although the regional distribution of the U.S. population has varied somewhat by age, the proportion of southerners in the total adult population is a sufficiently accurate estimate of the proportion in each birth cohort. (Of course, if the analysis is restricted to whites, the proportion of adult whites who were southerners at or near the time of each survey should be used for standardization.) Adjustment is accomplished by standardizing the responses by region to the correct, or approximately correct, regional distribution for the cohort at the time of the survey. Suppose, for instance, that 10 percent of the southerners chose a certain response alternative and that 50 percent of the nonsoutherners did so. Suppose also that the sample shows 10 percent of the cohort members to be southerners whereas the estimated correct percentage is about 25. In this case, the unadjusted data will show that 46 percent of the cohort members chose the response alternative. The adjusted percentage can be arrived at by a procedure which shows what the percentage would have been if southerners had been proportionately represented in the sample:

	Real Percentage of Cohort Members in Each Region		Percentage in Each Region Who Chose the Response Alternative		
Southerners	25	x	10	=	250
Nonsoutherners	75	x	50	=	3,750
Total	100				

Sum of the products = 4,000/100 = 40.0 (the adjusted percentage)

Adjustment for underrepresentation of low-education persons in the early cohort samples can be accomplished by an analogous standardization procedure, except that the educational distribution in one of the later samples can be used as the estimate of the correct distribution for all dates. (However, the survey used to estimate the correct distribution should not have been conducted when the cohort was so old that the sample size is very small.) For this adjustment, it is desirable to use at least four educational levels if the numbers of cases are sufficient, since use of broader levels will lead to "undercorrection" of the bias. If correction for underrepresentation of low-education persons makes a substantial difference, as it will in rare cases, the data probably contain substantial uncorrected bias due to underrepresentation of persons with low incomes and in occupations with low prestige. The adjustment on education will not remove most of this bias, since education is only moderately correlated with income and occupational prestige (Jencks, 1972). Little can be done about this remaining bias except to take it into account in interpreting the data, since the early opinion polls did not gather data on income, and many of the respondents had no occupation.

If, as is rarely the case, it seems necessary to adjust the data simultaneously for the underrepresentation of both southerners and low-education persons, the adjustment can be accomplished by using a multivariate classification of the responses and adjusting the data so that each category of the multivariate classification contributes to the adjusted percentage (or other adjusted estimate) in proportion to its representation in the total cohort population rather than in the sample. For instance, the categories used for standardization may include southerners with no more than eight years of school, nonsoutherners with no more than eight years of school, southerners with 8-11 years of school, and so forth. (In order to have a sufficient number of cases for reliable estimates of the dependent variable within each category, it may be necessary to use broader educational categories than when the adjustment involves education alone.)

As mentioned above, if cohort members who die young differ systematically on the dependent variable from those who survive, intracohort trends may result from mortality rather than from net change among the surviving cohort members. (Or, changes in the mean characteristics of surviving cohort members may be masked by the effects of mortality.) Such intracohort trends are real and not artifactual, but usually the cohort analyst is interested in the typical effects of aging on individuals rather than in intracohort change due to mortality. Doing separate analyses for males and females or standardizing the data for each cohort for each period to a sex ratio of 100 (as described above) will "adjust" the data for the declining sex ratio in the aging cohorts. However, other effects of differential mortality usually cannot be measured and definitively separated from the age and period effects with which they are confounded in the cohort diagonals of a cohort table or from the age and period effects with which they are confounded in the columns. Rather, one must estimate, with the assistance of any evidence at hand, the probable magnitude of mortality effects.

Fortunately, most nondemographic dependent variables of interest to cohort analysts are unlikely to correlate highly enough with longevity for there to be any important mortality effect. For instance, there is little reason to expect substantial mortality differences between persons with different political ideologies and orientations. On the other hand, important mortality effects are likely in the case of some dependent variables, such as measures of psychological well-being (see Palmore and Jeffers, 1971) and certain aspects of life styles, such as smoking and drinking. Therefore, it is advisable for the cohort analyst to become familiar with the known correlates of longevity, a good reference source being Palmore and Jeffers (1971).

If, on the basis of empirical evidence or theory, it seems likely that a dependent variable is correlated to an important degree with longevity, the cohort data should be interpreted with caution, since an accurate estimate of the mortality effect is not usually possible. It may be possible, however, to rule out mortality as the only or primary reason for an intracohort trend. For instance, Glenn and Zody (1970) found that as birth cohorts in the United States aged from young adulthood to middle age and from middle age to advanced maturity from 1945 to 1960, there was a decrease in the percentage of persons who said they drank alcoholic beverages in Gallup samples drawn from the cohorts. For instance, during this period, the 15-year cohort which was 20-34 years old in 1945 experienced, according to the data, a 4.2 point decline in the sex-standardized percentage of drinkers, the cohort 35-49 years old in 1945 experienced an 11.1 point decline, and the cohort 50-54 years old experienced a 12.1

point decline. Assuming that the change in each cohort represents the typical decline experienced by cohorts at that stage of aging, the data suggest that a cohort would typically experience a decline of almost 30 points in percentage of drinkers from ages 20-34 to ages 65-79—and at least a 20-point decline from the 20s to the 60s. Since there is reason to suspect that at least the heavier drinkers experienced greater mortality than the nondrinkers at each stage of aging, Glenn and Zody hypothesized that some of the intracohort decline in percentage of drinkers was a mortality effect. However, from recent vital statistics, they found that in recent birth cohorts in the United States, attrition through mortality from age 20 to age 60 has been less than 20 percent. Through a series of simple calculations, they were able to show that even if nondrinkers had experienced only half of their proportionate share of deaths, differential mortality would account for less than four points of the presumed 20 point decline from the 20s to the 60s. And even if all nondrinkers had lived and all deaths had occurred among drinkers, mortality would have reduced the percentage of drinkers by only about 7.5 points.

A final problem of comparability to be discussed here grows out of the fact that in the case of some series of repeated questions suitable for cohort analyses, some of the surveys have "weighted" samples and some do not. The weighted samples contain more than one card (or card image if the data are on tape) for some respondents, the purpose of the weighting being to correct for underrepresentation of some kinds of persons in the sample. For instance, the American Gallup data sets for 1960-1967 obtained from the Roper Center are usually weighted to correct for underrepresentation of both low-education persons and the kinds of persons who were rarely at home during the hours (early evening) when the interviews were conducted; thus, the sets contain about twice as many cards (or card images) as there are respondents in the samples. The weighted data should ordinarily be more representative of the population than the unweighted data, but weighting causes problems for significance testing by inflating the number of cases above the number of respondents. Since the results of significance tests with these data are in any event only roughly correct, estimating the number of respondents for subsamples seems justifiable and has been widely practiced, but of course it is important not to use the inflated number of cases for significance tests. (For the purist, there is a complicated procedure for "reweighting" the samples to arrive at the correct number of cases to use in significance tests; see Newman, 1975). Or, to avoid the problem of inflated numbers of cases and to make the data more nearly comparable with Gallup data gathered before 1960 and after 1967 (the latter of which can be weighted by the researcher by the use of weighting codes on the unweighted sets), the cohort analyst may wish to use unweighted data for all dates—which is easily done since there is a code which allows the researcher to access only the original, unweighted deck. Fortunately, the results of cohort analyses are usually virtually the same with the weighted and unweighted data.

PROBLEMS OF RANDOM SAMPLING ERROR

Much of the variation in the typical cohort table based on survey sample data is random sampling variation, and there is a danger that the cohort analyst will derive substantive conclusions from differences and patterns which reflect sampling error rather than differences and patterns in the population from which the samples were drawn.

Readers familiar with basic statistics and survey research methods will know that tests for statistical significance are the usual means for dealing with sampling error in survey data. If, for instance, a difference between two percentages is found to be significant at the .05 level, the probability that a difference that large would have resulted from random sampling error if there were no difference in the population is .05 or smaller. Therefore, one can be rather confident that a real difference existed in the population (but can be less confident that it was as large as the difference in the sample).

Techniques for using significance tests to deal with sampling variability in cohort tables constructed from survey sample data are not well developed, and most cohort analyses with survey sample data, including most of the better ones, have made little of no use of significance tests. The reasons are several, and a few warrant detailed discussion.

A "standard" cohort table shows the multivariate association of age and period (time) with the dependent variable, and if the association is not statistically significant (according, for instance, to a chi square test), then the variation in the table should be interpreted with caution, since the probability is rather high that it resulted to a large extent from sampling variability. Nevertheless, one must not conclude in such a case that in the total population there is not (and has not been) important variation among the categories represented by the cells of the table. Even in the absence of overall statistical significance, some patterns of variation in the table are due respect, including

(1) patterns predicted by hypotheses well-grounded in theory,
(2) monotonic, or almost monotonic, variation in a row, column, or cohort diagonal,

(3) patterns common to several rows, columns, or cohort diagonals, and

(4) patterns similar to those shown by other cohort studies with the same or similar dependent variables.

If a test shows that the overall association between a dependent variable and age and/or period is significant, the meaning is ambiguous, since it is not usually clear just what aspect of the variation is worthy of interpretation. If the sample sizes for the cells were equal, that would help, since one could have the greatest confidence in the largest differences between pairs of cell values. However, the number of cases in the cells usually varies considerably, always being smallest for the oldest age levels, for instance. Therefore, even when one can be rather confident that the overall associations between age and the dependent variable and between period and the dependent variable did not result from sampling error, one cannot be equally confident that apparently important patterns of variation in the table did not result largely or entirely from sampling error.

An additional difficulty is that significance tests designed for simple random samples do not yield accurate results when applied to national survey data, since national samples are never simple random samples. The drawing of a simple random sample requires a complete listing of the individuals in the population to be sampled, and there is no such listing of any national population. Therefore, national samples are always quota control samples (described above) or are multiple-stage "cluster" samples (described below), in which the sampling is random at all or most of the stages. In either case, the typical sampling error will be greater than with simple random samples of the same size, and, to further complicate matters, will not be consistent among different variables on the same survey or even for the same variable across surveys. All too often, users of national survey data (including authors of articles in major social science journals) simply apply the significance tests designed for simple random samples (which are routinely computed by many of the standard "package" computer programs) and fail to consider that the results are inaccurate. The more cautious researchers apply some kind of rule-of-thumb correction to all significance test results and are sensitive to the fact that even the "corrected" results may be in error by a substantial margin. (Accurate significance test results can be computed from "full probability" national samples, but only by a process too laborious and expensive for routine use—see Kish, 1965.) Why the corrections are necessary and why even the corrected significance levels (probabilities) must be viewed with caution will be apparent only after a brief description of the design of national survey samples.

The quota control samples (described above) used for the early national surveys were not randomly drawn at any stage of the sampling process; thus, any application of significance tests to data from these samples is problematic. However, Stephan and McCarthy (1958) estimate the sampling variance (standard errors) of estimates from the typical quota samples to be around 1.5 to 1.6 times the standard errors with simple random samples of the same size. Therefore, a crude estimate of the standard errors of estimates from quota samples can be arrived at by multiplying the standard errors computed by the formulae designed for simple random samples by 1.5 or 1.6. Although such a procedure may offend the sensibilities of statistical purists, its use may often be preferable to the likely alternatives, namely, ignoring sampling error or making even cruder guesses as to the magnitude of the error.

Common sense should be used in applying this, as any, rule-of-thumb correction. For reasons detailed below, a correction factor larger than 1.5 or 1.6 should be used in the case of any dependent variable on which there is known to be, or is likely to be, a high degree of residential segregation— as will be the case with any dependent variable strongly associated with size of community. Furthermore, if the percentages (or other estimates) have been adjusted for underrepresentation of southerners and/or low-education person by the procedures described above, a larger correction factor should be used. The reason is that the adjustment increases the contribution of relatively small population segments, in which estimates are relatively unstable, to the estimate for the cohort as a whole, thus increasing the latter's variability (instability). Experience with a limited number of series of adjusted estimates from surveys conducted within a short period of time suggests that the error variance may be as high as 1.8 or 2.0 times that with estimates from simple random samples (Glenn, 1970).

Almost all recent (since the mid-1950s) national surveys have used either "full probability" or "modified probability" samples with a multiple—stage cluster design. In either case, the United States (or other nation) is divided into a number of geographic areas, these areas in the U.S. usually being Standard Metropolitan Statistical Areas (SMSAs) and areas containing rural and small-town residents whose numbers are similar to the number of residents of the smaller SMSAs. A sample of these areas is drawn,[8] a team of interviewers is recruited and trained in each area drawn, and it is designated a *primary sampling unit* (PSU). Each PSU is usually small enough so that a team of interviewers can cover it without spending nights away from home. Since it would be prohibitively expensive to redraw PSUs for each survey, each survey organization uses the same sample of PSUs for a number of surveys, sometimes gradually replacing the PSUs over a period of years and sometimes completely redrawing the PSUs at regular intervals. Each PSU is divided into smaller geographic units, usually city blocks and segments of the countryside containing about as many people as the typical city block. For each survey, a random sample of these smaller units is drawn. The next stage differs according to whether the sample is "full probability" or "modified probability." In the former case, a random sample (or a close approximation thereof) of the households in each block or rural segment is drawn. The final stage, selection of respondents (persons to be interviewed) within the sampled households, differs according to the purpose of the survey. Some surveys are designed to be representative of households, not of individuals, in which case information is often obtained on all household members or on all adults. Most attitudinal surveys, however, aim to represent individuals, and thus the respondent may be chosen randomly from the adults in the household or may be selected by some predesignated formula. Modified probability sampling does not randomly select households or individuals but rather uses a quota method for selecting respondents within each block or rural segment included in the sample. However, this quota sampling differs from that used for the early "quota control" samples, insofar as the interviewers must follow a set procedure in selecting respondents and are allowed no discretion; hence, biases resulting from interviewer discretion are avoided.

Many recent academic surveys—including most of those conducted by the University of Michigan Survey Research Center and many of those conducted by the National Opinion Research Center—have used full probability samples. In contrast, commercial opinion polls and some academic surveys, such as the first three of the General Social Surveys, have used modified probability samples. Presumably, the standard errors of estimates from full probability samples tend to be somewhat smaller than those from modified probability samples, and the chance of systematic bias should be less with the former. Whereas full probability samples are clearly to be preferred, sampling experts do not agree on the extent to which they are superior to modified probability samples. They do agree, however, that with both kinds of samples, the standard errors are typically larger than those with simple random samples of the same size, the magnitude of the difference depending on how highly the variable of interest is correlated with the sample clusters (that is, with the PSUs, city blocks, and other "clusters" of individuals sampled at various stages). If the correlation is small, the error variance of estimates from cluster samples may be almost the same as that with simple random samples. However, sampling experts at the University of Michigan Survey Research Center have found a few variables so highly correlated with the sample clusters that the "cluster effect" inflated their standard errors fourfold (Glenn, 1975b). Fortunately, one usually has some a priori knowledge concerning the correlation of variables with the sample clusters. For instance, it is known that there is considerable residential segregation on the basis of occupation, race, income, and, by definition, community size. Therefore, any variable highly correlated with one of these variables will also be correlated with the sample clusters. For most variables of interest to cohort analysts, however, the correlation with the sample clusters is likely to be moderate, and thus multiplying the standard errors (for simple random samples) by 1.25 or 1.3 should usually be sufficient correction for the "cluster effect."

Although there was no random sampling of well-defined population clusters in the case of the "quota control" samples, they also had a kind of cluster effect. As a matter of convenience, each interviewer tended to select respondents from a restricted geographic area; thus with quota samples as well as the multistage cluster samples, a larger correction factor should be used for variables on which there is known to be, or on which there is likely to be, a high degree of residential segregation.

At best, use of significance tests with national survey data involves a great deal of guessing and use of rather crude rule-of-thumb corrections. Therefore, all significance test results should be viewed tentatively and should never be interpreted mechanically, as is all too often the case in social scientific reports of research with national survey data.

Although significance tests may not be very helpful to the cohort analyst in dealing with problems of sampling error, the problems can often be minimized by other procedures. For instance, in the case of the Gallup series of questions, it is often possible to pool the data from a large number of surveys conducted within a short period of time (a year or two) to increase the size of the cohort samples and reduce sampling variability. For instance, in a cohort analysis of political party identification with American Gallup data, the mean sample size for 10-year cohorts is 1,232 (Glenn, 1972); it would have been possible to have achieved a considerably larger mean sample size by using more surveys. For most purposes, it is desirable to use 10-year or smaller birth cohorts to detect with more precision just at what age levels changes occurred, but the sample size can be increased, and useful cohort studies can still be conducted, if 15-year or even 20-year cohorts are used (Glenn and Zody, 1970). Furthermore, problems of sampling error are greatly reduced if data are available for several points in time rather than just two or three. For instance, cohort samples with the SRC Election Studies are always rather small, but for some variables, data are available for 10 points in time. If there is a monotonic, or very nearly monotonic, intracohort (or intercohort) trend over 10 points in time, one needs neither significance tests nor large cohort samples to know that there is a very small probability of such a trend appearing in sample data if there were no trend in the population.

ANALYSIS AND INTERPRETATION

If possible, any cohort analysis should be begun by construction of a "standard" cohort table (or tables), that is, a table in which the intervals between dates for which there are data are the same as the intervals used to delineate the cohorts (for instance, see Tables 1 and 2). However, it often will not be possible to construct a standard table since the intervals between the surveys for which data are available will be uneven, or else the surveys will be spaced too far apart or too close together for a standard table to provide cohorts sufficiently narrow to be useful or sufficiently wide to have samples large enough for reliable estimates of the dependent variable. In such cases, two tables should be constructed for each dependent variable, one in which each cohort can be traced through time by reading across a row (as in Tables 3, 4, and 5) and one in which comparable sets of cross-sectional data are juxtaposed, as in a standard cohort table (see Table 6). The second table provides trend data for each age level; if the intervals between dates are equal, the trend data for the youngest adult age level may provide clues, in a manner discussed below, for a tentative separation of the age and period effects confounded in the intracohort trend data.

TABLE 4

Percentage of Respondents Who Said They Did Not Drink Alcoholic Beverages,[1] in Three 15-Year Cohorts, 1945 through 1960 (Ns are in parentheses)

	Year			
	1945	1950	1955	1960
Cohort 1--Age:	20-34	25-39	30-34	35-39
	26.1 (937)	33.5 (499)	31.4 (586)	30.3 (439)
Cohort 2--Age:	35-49	40-54	45-59	50-64
	31.8 (1,049)	44.9 (380)	41.1 (414)	42.9 (372)
Cohort 3--Age:	50-64	55-69	60-74	65-79
	42.8 (676)	53.7 (253)	60.8 (207)	54.9 (221)

Source: American Institute of Public Opinion (American Gallup) Surveys 360, 450, 543, and 622. Adapted from Glenn and Zody (1970).

[1]Standardized to a sex ratio of 100 and to the educational distribution shown by the 1960 data.

TABLE 5

Percentage of Respondents Who Said They Approved of
Admission of Communist China to the United Nations,[1] in
10-Year Cohorts, 1954 to 1969
(Ns are in parentheses)

	Year					
	1954	1957	1958	1964[2]	1965[2]	1969
Cohort 1--Age:				20-29	21-30	25-34
				30.2	29.8	38.3
				(1,115)	(1,252)	(273)
Cohort 2--Age:	20-29	23-32	24-33	30-39	31-40	35-44
	7.3	19.8	23.7	21.2	26.8	35.3
	(332)	(330)	(554)	(1,156)	(1,339)	(313)
Cohort 3--Age:	30-39	33-42	34-43	40-49	41-50	45-54
	8.4	14.4	18.6	18.8	19.7	32.8
	(403)	(381)	(661)	(1,308)	(1,452)	(289)
Cohort 4--Age:	40-49	43-52	44-53	50-59	51-60	55-64
	5.9	14.0	20.9	14.8	18.1	24.7
	(359)	(275)	(561)	(1,127)	(1,161)	(236)
Cohort 5--Age:	50-59	53-62	54-63	60-69	61-70	65-74
	6.1	9.8	16.9	9.4	19.0	26.9
	(220)	(223)	(433)	(890)	(1,056)	(168)
Cohort 6--Age:	60-69	63-72	64-73	70-79	71-80	75-84
	5.0	10.1	11.5	9.1	15.4	17.1
	(163)	(149)	(343)	(530)	(453)	(100)

Source: American Institute of Public Opinion (American Gallup) Surveys 533, 534,
578, 594, 650, 684, 701, 706, 721, and 774.

[1] Standardized to a sex ratio of 100 and to the educational distribution shown by
the 1964 data.

[2] Weighted Ns.

Regardless of the purpose of the cohort analysis, the researcher will
usually approach the data with certain hypotheses which predict certain
patterns of variation (or lack of variation) in the cohort table. For instance,
if the dependent variable is some measure of conservatism and if the hypothesis is that aspects of the aging process lead to an increase in conservatism, the researcher would expect (in the absence of offsetting cohort and
period effects) that the older people at each period will be more conservative, as an aggregate, than the younger people and that the trend in each
aging cohort will be toward conservatism. In this case, the next step of the
study after construction of the cohort table (with the accompanying table
reporting comparable sets of cross-sectional data, if necessary) should be a
careful inspection of the table (or tables) to see if it (or they) exhibits, or
approximates, the pattern of variation which would occur if all of the

TABLE 6

Percentage of Respondents Who Said They Approved of Admission of Communist China to the United Nations,[1] by Age, 1954 to 1969

(Ns are in parentheses)

				Year		
Age	1954	1957	1958	1964[2]	1965[2]	1969
20-29	7.3 (332)	17.0 (256)	23.7 (422)	30.2 (1,115)	29.5 (1,145)	46.9 (261)
30-39	8.4 (403)	18.5 (374)	21.9 (670)	21.2 (1,156)	26.8 (1,318)	36.2 (286)
40-49	5.9 (359)	12.9 (315)	21.4 (585)	18.8 (1,308)	19.0 (1,413)	36.1 (329)
50-59	6.1 (220)	10.6 (236)	18.2 (493)	14.8 (1,127)	18.0 (1,181)	30.6 (257)
60-69	5.0 (163)	7.4 (186)	12.9 (392)	9.4 (890)	16.6 (1,133)	26.1 (206)
70-79	5.0 (121)	5.3 (70)	11.8 (211)	9.1 (530)	15.1 (487)	24.6 (117)

Source: American Institute of Public Opinion (American Gallup) Surveys 533, 534, 578, 594, 650, 684, 701, 706, 721, and 774.

[1] Standardized to a sex ratio of 100.

[2] Weighted Ns.

variation in the table were due to the hypothesized age effects. If so, the data suggest that the hypothesis is correct, although, for reasons explained below, they do not definitively confirm it.

On other occasions, the hypothesis may predict variation in the cohort table due to cohort effects or period effects. Therefore, the cohort analyst should know how to "eyeball" or visually inspect a cohort table to detect the pattern of variation which would occur if

    (1) all of the variation were due to age effects,

    (2) all of the variation were due to cohort effects, and

    (3) all of the variation were due to period effects.

Mason, Mason, Winsborough, and Poole (1973) present tables of hypothetical data showing pure age effects, pure cohort effects, and pure period effects. Rather than reproduce those tables here, I present a different but similar set of tables (Tables 7, 8, and 9) so that the interested student can examine two sets of tables to gain greater sensitivity to the patterns one should try to detect in cohort data.

TABLE 7
Cohort Table Showing Hypothetical Data (Percentages)
in Which All Variation is Due to Age Effects

	Year			
Age	1940	1950	1960	1970
20 – 29	40	40	40	40
30 – 39	45	45	45	45
40 – 49	50	50	50	50
50 – 59	55	55	55	55
60 – 69	60	60	60	60
70 – 79	65	65	65	65
Age-Adjusted Total[1]	52.5	52.5	52.5	52.5

[1]Standardized to an age distribution with an equal number of persons at each age level.

In a table showing "pure" age effects (see Table 7), each set of cross-sectional data will be identical. There will be the same pattern of variation down each column from the lower to the higher age levels and there will be no variation across the rows. In Table 7, each 10-year increment in age is associated with the same increment (five points) in the dependent variable; that is, the relationship between age and the dependent variable is *linear*. However, pure age effects need not be linear; they can be nonlinear in the sense that different 10-year increments of age are associated with different-sized increments in the dependent variable, or they can be *curvilinear* or *nonmonotonic*, in which case some increments of age are associated with increments in the dependent variable and some are associated with decrements. For instance, the values of the dependent variable may be higher in the middle age levels than in either the lower or higher levels. So long as the cross-sectional data are identical for different periods and there is no trend at each age level, the pattern is that predicted by pure age effects. Of course, in sample data, sampling error will produce some variation across the rows, so that a table which approximates the pattern predicted by pure age effects is evidence in support of hypothesized age effects.

TABLE 8
Cohort Table Showing Hypothetical Data (Percentages)
in Which All Variation is Due to Cohort Effects

Age	Year			
	1970	1950	1960	1970
20 - 29	50	40	30	20
30 - 39	60	50	40	30
40 - 49	70	60	50	40
50 - 59	80	70	60	50
60 - 69	90	80	70	60
70 - 79	100	90	80	70
Age-Adjusted Total[1]	75	65	55	45

[1] Standardized to an age distribution with an equal number of persons at each age level.

In a table in which all of the variation is due to cohort effects (see Table 8), there will be no variation in the cohort diagonals, and the variation from the younger to the older age levels will be opposite in direction from the variation from the earlier to the later periods at each age level. Although Table 8 shows a linear pattern of intercohort variation, the variation can be nonlinear and nonmonotonic. Whereas a pattern of pure age effects will produce no change in the level of the dependent variable in the total adult population except any change produced by changes in the age distribution, a pattern of pure cohort effects will produce change in the total population due to cohort succession (see the age-adjusted totals at the botton of Tables 7 and 8).

In a table in which all of the variation is due to period effects (see Table 9), there will be no variation by age at any period, and the variation from each period to the next will be the same at each age level and in each cohort. Furthermore, there will be change in the level of the dependent variable in the total adult population equal to the change at each age level and in each cohort.

TABLE 9
Cohort Table Showing Hypothetical Data (Percentages)
in Which All Variation is Due to Period Effects

Age	Year			
	1940	1950	1960	1970
20 – 29	70	60	50	40
30 – 39	70	60	50	40
40 – 49	70	60	50	40
50 – 59	70	60	50	40
60 – 69	70	60	50	40
70 – 79	70	60	50	40
Age-Adjusted Total[1]	70	60	50	40

[1]Standardized to an age distribution with an equal number of people at each level. In this table, the age-adjusted total equals the unadjusted total.

The reader may suspect that in actual data, patterns predicted by pure age, cohort, or period effects will rarely occur. It is true that in most cohort tables, there is evidence for at least two of the kinds of effects. However, cohort tables showing or approximating the pattern predicted by pure age effects are surprisingly frequent, an example being Table 4. Tables with the pattern predicted by pure period effects *are* rare, and I have never seen a cohort table with an attitudinal or behavioral dependent variable which shows the pattern of variation predicted by pure cohort effects (although a table in which amount of formal education is the dependent variable will exhibit such a pattern).

As I stressed earlier, there are at least two possible explanations for the pattern of variation in any cohort table, and a table showing the pattern of variation predicted by pure age, cohort, or period effects is no exception. For instance, in the case of Table 7, influences associated with aging could have produced all of the variation, but the variation could also have been produced by a combination of influences associated with cohort membership and period. For instance, a cohort table with American data in which job satisfaction is the dependent variable will exhibit a pattern similar to that in Table 7 if the measure of job satisfaction is sensitive enough to capture the positive association of job satisfaction with age.[9] The cross-sectional data for the different periods will be almost identical, and the level of job satisfaction in the total employed population will vary little through time. Obviously, this pattern could reflect pure age effects, that is, workers may typically experience an increase in job satisfaction as they grow older due to influences associated with the aging process. However, in this case, there is a plausible as well as a possible alternative explanation. In recent years, each cohort which matured into adulthood may have had early socialization which made its members typically less inclined to enjoy work than the members of the older cohorts. That this may be true is suggested by the large speculative literature dealing with an alleged decline in the "Protestant work ethic" in this country in recent years (see Whyte, 1956). Such an intercohort trend, by itself, would have produced a decline in the level of job satisfaction in the total work force (as well as a positive association of job satisfaction with age at each period), and no such decline occurred. However, the overall effects of the intercohort trend may have been offset by changes in period influences—such as changes in styles of supervision and increased efforts by employers and managers to increase morale and job satisfaction—which tended to increase job satisfaction.

Fortunately for cohort analysts, there usually is only one *plausible* explanation for a pattern of variation predicted by pure age, cohort, or period effects. For instance, the only convincing explanation for the data in Table 4 is that they show largely age effects, since in the case of drinking—as in the case of most dependent variables—it seems highly improbable that trends in period and cohort effects will offset one another so as to leave the level in the total adult population almost constant. Rather, the two trends usually result from the same basic influences and thus tend to reinforce rather than offset one another in their effects on trends in the total adult population. For instance, any changes in preadult socialization which would produce a trend in drinking habits among cohorts maturing into adulthood are likely to result from influences which also impinge on persons who are already adults and which therefore tend to produce changes among adult individuals in the same direction as the intercohort trend.

The fact that cohort and period effects are often not causally distinct—in the sense that they do not result in different-signed effects on the level of the dependent variable in the total adult population—can also be useful for estimation of age effects when the pattern of variation is more complicated than that predicted by pure age effects. When, on the basis of theory and common sense, it seems likely that the trends in cohort and period effects have resulted from the same influences, the trend in the young adult age level (for instance, ages 18-24, or 20-29) can be used to estimate the nature of the influences for change, other than those associated with aging, which have impinged on members of the aging cohorts. For instance, if, in such a case, intracohort trends and the trend in the young adult age level are in opposite directions, it is reasonable to attribute the intracohort trends to influences associated with aging. If, on the other hand, intracohort trends and the trend in the young adult age level are in the same direction, the evidence is more ambiguous. However, if both have resulted from the same set of influences, the change in the young adult age level should usually be greater than that in the cohorts, since the change in the young adult age level reflects cohort succession as well as the response of individuals to period influences. Therefore, greater but same-signed change in the cohorts than in the young adult age level is tentative evidence for age effects.

How influences for change which impinge on aging cohorts can be estimated from changes in the dependent variable at the young adult age level can be illustrated with some simple computations from the data in Tables 5 and 6 (see Table 10). The upward trend in the 20-29 age level in percentage of respondents who said they approved of admission of Communist

TABLE 10

Changes in Percentage of Respondents Who Said They Approved of Admission of Communist China to the United Nations, in the 20-29 Age Range and in Each of Five 10-Year Birth Cohorts, 1954 to 1958, 1958 to 1965, and 1965 to 1969

	Period		
	1954 to 1958	1958 to 1965	1965 to 1969
20-29 Age Range	+16.4	+ 5.8	+17.4
Cohort 2	+16.4	+ 3.1	+ 8.5
Cohort 3	+10.2	+ 1.1	+13.1
Cohort 4	+15.0	- 2.8	+ 6.6
Cohort 5	+10.8	+ 2.1	+ 7.9
Cohort 6	+ 6.5	+ 3.9	+ 1.7
Mean Change in Cohorts	+11.8	+ 1.5	+ 7.6

Source: Computed from data in Tables 5 and 6.

China to the United Nations strongly suggests that from 1954 to 1958, from 1958 to 1965, and from 1965 to 1969 the period influences were generally conducive to development of more favorable or more tolerant attitudes toward Communist China. The trend was also toward "approval" in each of the five birth cohorts, but since the intercohort shifts were in no case greater than the change at the 20-29 age level, and in all but one case were smaller, it does not seem reasonable to attribute any of the intra-cohort change to influences associated with aging. Since, generally speaking, the change was less in the older than in the younger cohorts, influences associated with aging may have offset to some degree the period influences. If so, the offsetting influences may have resulted from those aspects of aging which are alleged to be conducive to conservatism (Glenn, 1974), or, more likely, from a tendency for aging persons to become less susceptible to attitudinal change. Still another possible interpretation is that the members of the older cohorts were less susceptible to change not because of their age but because of characteristics resulting from their cohort membership. Choice among these alternative interpretations must be made on the basis of theory and side information and must be tentative. However, the comparison of intracohort change with change at the 20-29 age level allows a rather confident rejection of an aging explanation of the intracohort change.

Quite often a cohort analysis is motivated by knowledge of an association in cross-sectional data between age and some dependent variable. Since such an association could reflect age effects, cohorts effects, or a mixture of the two, a cohort analysis is undertaken to help decide among the three alternative interpretations. If both age and period effects seem to be present, the researcher will be interested in the relative importance of the two kinds of effects.

For reasons recently spelled out in detail by Philip Converse (1976), the task of deciding on the relative importance of age and cohort effects can be very difficult if, as is often the case, the magnitude of the association of age with the dependent variable is rather small. Explaining why this is true requires brief discussion of a more general issue relating to cross-tabular analysis.

A common mistake among researchers who examine cross-tabular data and interpret differences between percentages is to "overinterpret" rather small differences.[10] For instance, if a researcher finds a 12 to 15 point difference in the dependent variable between extreme categories of the independent variable, the researcher is likely to conclude that the association between the two variables is "moderate" or even "strong." In contrast, a researcher who uses regression techniques or a "proportional-reduction-in-error" measure of association on the same data will probably conclude that the association is weak. The tendency to "overinterpret" a rather small percentage difference may be enhanced if the researcher is steeped in a literature which has discussed the association as though it were strong and important.

Whereas an "overinterpretation" of a weak or modest association is usually just a matter of misplaced emphasis, in cohort analysis it can lead to patently incorrect conclusions. Since the difference in age between the oldest and youngest cohorts included in one study is usually 40 years or more, the cohort analyst may overlook the fact that a difference of a few percentage points (on the dependent variable) between the youngest and oldest cohorts can be explained by a very weak aging effect during the typical year, or even the typical decade, of the aging process—so weak that the trend in any one cohort diagonal, or cohort row, is likely to be obscured by sampling variability. Therefore, the cohort analyst may conclude that there are no apparent age effects even when such effects totally account for the cross-sectional age variation of the dependent variable.

For an apparent example of such a misinterpretation, I turn to one of my own cohort studies. In an attempt to understand the sources of the increase in political independence during the late 1960s, I computed intra-cohort trend data from Gallup polls conducted from 1945 to 1971 (Glenn, 1972). As an incidental part of the study, I addressed the question as to whether the negative association between age and independence shown by the data from the 1940s and 1950s reflected cohort effects or whether it reflected an effect of aging. For this purpose, I concentrated on the period from 1945 to 1957, since during that time the lack of a discernible trend in percentage of independents at the 20-29 age level suggested that there were no important period influences either for or against independence (see Table 11). Therefore, I assumed that any important effects of age on independence would be reflected in readily apparent intracohort trends. (The sampling variability was less than in most cohort studies, since the mean cohort N was 1,010.) Examination of the data revealed no consistent intracohort trends (of the 15 intracohort changes from one date to the next, seven were up and eight were down); thus I concluded that there was no convincing evidence for age effects and that the age variation in independence apparently reflected an earlier (before 1945) intercohort trend toward independence. This conclusion is widely cited in the literature, and the paraphrases of it generally make it appear less tentative than my original wording.

The data in Table 11 *do* strongly suggest that any influence of aging on independence was rather weak, at most. However, I failed to consider that only a rather weak effect in each cohort during the 12-year period covered by the study would be sufficient to produce the cross-sectional difference

TABLE 11
Percentage of Independents in the 20-29 Age Range and
in Five 10-Year Birth Cohorts,[1] 1945 to 1957
(Ns are in parentheses)

	Year			
	1945	1949	1953	1957
20-29 Age Range	25.6 (649)	23.1 (1,602)	25.8 (1,316)	23.4 (1,035)
Cohort 1--Age:	20-29	24-33	28-37	32-41
	25.6 (649)	21.4 (1,909)	22.6 (1,520)	23.0 (1,536)
Cohort 2--Ages:	30-39	34-43	28-37	32-41
	17.6 (666)	19.4 (2,046)	20.2 (1,321)	19.0 (1,287)
Cohort 3--Ages:	40-49	44-53	48-57	52-61
	19.8 (662)	19.7 (1,727)	21.2 (1,114)	17.0 (943)
Cohort 4--Ages:	50-59	54-63	58-67	62-71
	16.1 (490)	17.9 (1,209)	18.1 (750)	16.9 (672)
Cohort 5--Ages:	60-69	64-73	68-77	72-81
	20.0 (307)	13.8 (727)	13.4 (382)	13.1 (291)

Source: American Institute of Public Opinion (American Gallup) Surveys 377, 432, 433, 434, 521, 523, 524, 578, 580, 582, and 587. Adapted from Table 2 in Glenn (1972).

[1] Standardized to a sex ratio of 100 and to the education distribution shown for the cohorts by data collected in 1965 (cohorts 1 through 4) or 1961 (cohort 5).

in percentage of independents between the oldest and youngest cohorts (mean for the four dates = 8.1 percentage points). Specifically, the required annual rate of decrease was about 0.2 percentage points, or about 2.4 points every 12 years. In fact, according to the data, the mean annual change in percentage of independents in the five cohorts was −.16—four-fifths of the required change. Therefore, it seems likely that effects of aging accounted for most of the age variation in independence, and in view of sampling error, they may well have accounted for all of it.[11]

The lesson is clear: before the researcher uses intracohort trend data to interpret a cross-sectional pattern of age variation in a dependent variable, he or she should compute the annual rate of intracohort change needed to account for all of the variation. Since the association of age with most dependent variables is rather weak, the required rate of intracohort change will usually be rather small—in which cases the researcher may be able to make no confident conclusions about the relative importance of age and cohort effects. If the age variation departs markedly from linearity (an equal increment or decrement associated with each year of age), the non-linearity should be taken into account. For instance, if the dependent variable is almost constant from young adulthood to middle age but varies directly with age above a certain level, one needs to compute the required annual rate of change from the age level at which the positive association begins.

"Rigorous" Methods for Estimating Age, Cohort, and Period Effects

The methods described in the preceeding paragraphs are rather simple and informal and thus will not satisfy researchers who believe that social scientific research—if it is to be truly scientific—must use only the most rigorous available methods. Some researchers eschew the simple methods out of fear of appearing unsophisticated, and thus their research becomes a conspicuous display of technical expertise. A rule of thumb conductive to good research (if not always to successful status striving) is that research methods should never be more complicated than is necessary for the problem at hand. The results of simpler research are more easily communicated, and simpler methods are more likely to be well understood even by the researcher. Package computer programs have made the mechanics of applying complicated methods rather easy, but there has been no corresponding increase in the ease with which researchers can gain understanding of the logic of the techniques and the ability to interpret the results intelligently.

Nevertheless, there are now few kinds of research for which an exclusive reliance on "eyeballing" and simple manipulation of cross-tabular data can be justified, even when the sole purpose is description. If, as I maintain, cohort analysis can, at this stage in its development, benefit little from application of the available "rigorous" techniques, then it differs from most other kinds of social scientific research. This uniqueness which I attribute to cohort analysis will engender skepticism in some readers, so I must defend my point of view. In order to do so, I must briefly describe the more rigorous methods of cohort analysis.

Most of the more rigorous methods in some way involve *statistical interaction*, which occurs when the relationship between two variables depends on the value or values of one or more additional variables. For instance, the relationship between age and reported happiness depends on gender, that is, it differs between males and females. This is an example of a *zero-order interaction*. Furthermore, the extent of the male-female difference in the relationship between age and reported happiness—or the degree of the zero-order interaction—differs between blacks and whites. This is an example of a *first-order interaction*. If the degree or nature of this first-order interaction were to depend on the value of yet another variable, such as region, there would be a *second-order interaction,* and so forth.

There are a number of statistical techniques which may be used to measure and test for the statistical significance of interactions. I need not describe those techniques here, but they include analysis of variance, analysis of covariance, dummy variable regression analysis, and Goodman's log-linear analysis (Iversen and Norpoth, 1976; Blalock, 1972; Goodman, 1972).

Some rigorous methods of cohort analysis, including especially those used by developmental psychologists, are based on the assumption that age effects will appear as an interaction between cohort and period, that cohort effects will appear an an interaction between age and period, and that period effects will appear as an interaction between cohort and age. Whether or not this assumption is correct can be revealed by close inspection of Tables 7, 8, and 9, which show patterns predicted by pure age, cohort, and period effects. Table 8 is easiest to inspect for interaction, since the interaction would be between age and period and thus could be detected by comparisons among the rows and comparisons among the columns. If cohort effects necessarily appear as interactions between age and period, the association of period with the dependent variable should vary among the age levels, and the association of age with the dependent variable should vary among the periods. More specifically, the pattern of variation of the dependent variable should vary among both the rows and the columns.

The expected variation is not present.[13] Interaction, in the usual sense of that term, does not appear in the table, and the standard statistical tests for interaction would not detect the cohort effects (see Iversen and Norpoth, 1976, for discussion of one of the tests).

I need not discuss Tables 7 and 9, but inspection of them yields the same results. From these results one can surmise that *linear* age, cohort, and period effects will not appear as interactions detectable by statistical tests for interaction. Nonlinear effects will involve interactions, as the reader can determine by constructing hypothetical tables showing nonlinear age, cohort, and period effects. However, the interaction will reflect only the extent of the nonlinearity, not the magnitude of the effects. Even the interactions reflecting nonlinearity in age, cohort, and period effects are of limited utility to cohort analysts, since there is no empirical way to distinguish between interactions which are aspects of age, cohort, and period effects and those which are not. For instance, not all interactions between age and period are aspects of cohort effects.[13]

A "sophisticated" technique of cohort analysis even more seductive than analysis of variance and other tests for interaction has been introduced by Mason, Mason, Winsborough, and Poole (1973). To describe the technique in detail would be to assume an unlikely degree of statistical knowledge on the part of most readers; suffice it to say that the technique is a form of dummy variable regression analysis which provides estimates of the effects on a dependent variable of each age level, cohort, and period, except that the effects of either two age levels, two cohorts, or two periods must be assumed to be equal. The necessity to assume that the effects of two categories are equal is not especially troublesome, since it is usually possible to make an assumption which is likely to be only a small distortion of reality. However, the technique also requires a much more troublesome assumption, namely, that the age, cohort, and period effects are additive (do not interact). That is, it must be assumed that age effects are the same for all cohorts and periods, that cohort effects are the same for all ages and periods, and that period effects are the same for all ages and cohorts. For many attitudinal and behavioral dependent variables, this assumption is not realistic.

I have already discussed the widespread assumption that attitudes tend to become less responsive to influences for change as people grow older; if this assumption is correct, then period effects should *not*, as the additive model assumes, be the same for all age levels and all cohorts. Although there is no definitive empirical evidence in support of this assumption (see Glenn, 1974; Cutler and Kaufman, 1975, for some of the evidence), a great deal of theory suggests that it should be correct. The theory ranges from that dominant among contemporary developmental psychologists (see Botwinick, 1973) to that espoused by such earlier theorists as Karl Mannheim (1928). The reasons given for expecting attitudinal and behavioral rigidity to increase beyond adolescence or young adulthood include neurological change, decreased social and geographic mobility and consequent changes in social contacts, the accumulative effects of attempts to resolve cognitive dissonance, ego involvement in publicly espoused views, and the fact that the stimuli for change which impinge on older adults must overcome the accumulative effects of a larger number of previous stimuli than those which impinge on younger people. If, for any of these reasons, aging leads to decreased susceptibility to change, then influences for change from one period to another should have less effect on older people than on younger ones.

Somewhat different theoretical arguments against the additivity of age, cohort, and period effects are given by such authors as Ryder (1965) and Carlsson and Karlsson (1970), who suggest that the effects of membership in a given cohort are likely to vary through time. In spite of any tendency toward attitudinal rigidity which comes with aging, the "formative experiences" of each cohort continue into adulthood, and thus cohort effects will change as a result of each change in the unique situation of the cohort. To illustrate, a relatively small cohort (in terms of number of members), such as the one born in the United States during the Great Depression of the 1930s, typically has unusual economic and occupational opportunities when it first enters the labor market. However, for many if not most cohort members, this advantage is likely to cease or substantially diminish in middle age, when the more numerous and better educated (and perhaps less "spoiled") members of the younger cohorts become able to compete effectively, and when, as taxpapers, the initially advantaged cohort bears a major brunt of a high dependency ratio. Therefore, whatever effects economic advantage has on attitudes and behavior are likely to become smaller, and may even be reversed, as the cohort grows older.

In addition, the effects of growing older may differ substantially among birth cohorts. As I point above, the aging process has three major aspects, in addition to chronological aging—biological, psychological, and social—and only the first has been even approximately constant through time and from one society to another. In a rapidly changing society such as ours, the typical changes in personality and behavior (psychological aging) and in status and roles and in relations to other people (social aging) which accompany chronological aging may vary appreciably even among the cohorts represented in one cohort table. For instance, the cohort of females now in young adulthood differs markedly from cohorts only a few years older in capability for voluntary fertility control; its members are the first females able to plan and begin a career with high assurance that it will not be interrupted involuntarily by pregnancy. The consequences of this change for the traditional "family life cycle," and thus for many kinds of attitudes and behavior, may result in a quite different process of social and psychological aging than that experienced by previous cohorts.

If, as all of this theory suggests, the assumption of additivity of age, cohort, and period effects is rarely realistic in the case of nondemographic dependent variables, it follows that the estimates of effects provided by the Mason et al. method will rarely be accurate. They may sometimes be accurate, but it is difficult, if not impossible, to know when they are accurate and when they are not. To be sure, theory and various kinds of "side information" can be used to assess the probable validity of the assumption of additivity in the case of the dependent variable of interest, but in most cases it will be easier to use the side information to interpret simpler data.

I do not claim that rigorous methods of cohort analysis should never be used, since new methods are being developed which may overcome some of the limitations of the methods I have discussed. However, the cohort analyst should never plunge directly into a rigorous analysis without first applying the simpler methods, and the researcher should never forget that rigorous methods cannot overcome the fact that any set of cohort data is always susceptible to at least two interpretations (in terms of the kinds of effects reflected in it). Therefore, rigorous methods cannot diminish the need to use theory and various kinds of side information to interpret the data.

Methods to Study Change

Earlier, I briefly discussed the use of cohort analysis to study social, cultural, and political change, and I noted that the techniques for such study are not well developed. In view of the primitive stage of development of the techniques, I need only describe them briefly and point out their limitations.

Since change in a total population of a society, or in the total adult population, between any two points in time ordinarily results primarily from intracohort change and cohort succession, it would be useful for several purposes to allocate the change between those two sources. Furthermore, since cohort succession can be divided into (1) addition of new individuals and (2) substraction of individuals, it would also be useful to allocate the change due to cohort succession to the two component sources. In fact, however, it is impossible precisely to allocate change to these three sources—not simply because we lack well developed methods but because the effects of the different sources of change are not completely distinct. Instead of each source making a distinct, additive contribution to change, the different sources interact; that is, the contribution of each to change in the total population depends partly on the nature of the other sources. For instance, the contribution of intracohort change to change in the total adult population during a given decade depends partly on the numbers and characteristics of people who died and of people who aged into the adult population during that period. Therefore, any attempt at allocation can only provide rough estimates of the relative importance of the different sources. Even if better techniques of allocation are developed, as they no doubt eventually will be, some of the change will be left to be allocated to interactions between and among the sources rather than to specific sources.

As I point out above, the most theoretically useful definition of "change due to cohort succession" is that change due to permanent differences among the cohorts, excluding any change due to differences between exiting and entering individuals growing out of age and stage of the life cycle. However, since no existing cohort table traces any cohort (much less several) through its entire adult life span, it is impossible to deal with "change due to cohort succession" in this more useful sense. Instead, we perforce must deal with all change due to differences between exiting and entering individuals, regardless of whether those differences are cohort effects or age effects. However, as I have repeatedly stressed, theory and various kinds of "side information" can help the cohort analyst to decide which differences are cohort effects and which are age effects.

Most attempts to allocate change among its sources have utilized a method by which the value of the dependent variable which would have existed at time two if a certain source had been inoperative is computed and subtracted from the observed value at time two. The difference is the estimated contribution of that source to change in the total adult (or other) population between time one and time two. For instance, to estimate the contribution of intracohort change, one computes what the value of the dependent variable would have been at time two if no intracohort change had occurred. The procedure is a form of standardization, and the computation is simple. For each cohort for which there are data for both dates, the time one values are substituted in the time two age-cohort distribution and a hypothetical value for the entire population for time two is computed.

To illustrate this procedure, I draw upon the data on approval of admission of Communist China to the United Nations reported in Tables 5 and 6. For convenience, I deal with the population ages 20 through 79 rather than the total adult population, and I am concerned with the change from 1954 to 1964. The percentage approving in 1954 was 6.6 and in 1964 it was 18.4, for an increase of 11.8 points. To estimate how much of this change was due to intracohort change, I first compute the percentage distribution of the respondents among the six age levels in 1964 (column A below). Then, for the cohort ages 20-29, which was not in the population in 1954, I place the percentage approving as of 1964 in Column B of the table below. The other five age levels contained cohorts 2 through 6 in 1964, so for each of those cohorts I insert the percentage approving *as of 1954* in Column B. Then I multiply A by B at each age level, sum the products, and divide by 100 to arrive at the hypothetical percentage of approval responses in the total population in 1964 assuming no intracohort change from 1954 to 1964:

Age in 1964	Column A	Column B	Product of A and B
20-29	18.2	30.2	549.64
30-39	18.9	7.3	137.97
40-49	21.4	8.4	179.76
50-59	18.4	5.9	108.56
60-69	14.5	6.1	88.45
70-79	8.7	5.0	43.50

Sum of the Products = 1,107.88/100 = 11.1

When this hypothetical percentage is subtracted from the real percentage, the difference is 7.3—the estimated contribution of intracohort change.

By a strictly analogous procedure, one can estimate the contribution of cohort succession by computing what the approval percentage would have been for the population in 1964 if no cohort succession had occurred from 1954 to 1964 and by subtracting the hypothetical 1964 percentage from the real percentage. In the illustrative case, the estimated contribution is 3.3 points. Since the sum of the estimated contributions of intracohort change and cohort succession is only 10.6, just over a point of the observed change remains unallocated. However, the allocated change strongly suggests that intracohort change made a substantially greater contribution to change in the total population than did cohort succession.

The contributions of the two components of cohort succession, addition of individuals and subtraction of individuals, can each be estimated by procedures analogous to the one illustrated above. In each case, a hypothetical value for the dependent variable for the later date is computed by assuming that the source of change was inoperative from time one to time two, and then the hypothetical value is subtracted from the observed value. In the case of addition of individuals, the hypothetical value can be computed simply by removing the time two respondents representing cohorts who aged into adulthood between time one and time two and by computing the value without those respondents. Computing what the value of the dependent variable would have been in the total population if no mortality had occurred is more complicated, partly because it necessitates assuming what would have happened to the attitudes or behavior of persons who died between time one and time two if they had not died. Rather than describe the rather complex procedure, I recommend that the effects of subtraction of individuals (through death or aging out of the age range of the delineated population) be estimated by subtracting the estimated contribution of addition of individuals from the estimated contribution of both aspects of cohort succession. The resulting estimate may contain a small magnitude of change which should remain unallocated, but the usual error will be very small relative to sampling error.

Since sampling error will be substantial unless the samples are rather large, and since the estimates are subject to other sources of error, the estimated contributions of the components of change should be interpreted with caution. In spite of their crudeness, however, they are often useful. For instance, if they indicate that most of the observed change in the total population during a given period resulted from mortality, the influences ultimately responsible for the change will be found in historical data for earlier periods rather than in the events and circumstances of the period during which the measured change occurred. For instance, at least around half of the decline in Republican party identification during the two and a half decades after World War II apparently resulted from the dying off of the older cohorts, and thus ultimately resulted from the differential impact on the cohorts of the Great Depression of the 1930s (Glenn and Hefner, 1972).

Methods to Study the Susceptibility to Change of Aging Individuals

The most important cohort studies in the next few years are likely to deal with the issue of whether aging individuals tend to become so inflexible in their attitudes and behavior that they respond little or not at all to influences for change—or whether substantial change is even possible among the elderly. As I point out above, this issue is very important for both theoretical and practical reasons.

The methods appropriate for investigation of this issue might seem obvious; one needs to compare change in older and younger cohorts on various dependent variables during given periods of time. The "rigidity" hypothesis predicts greater change in younger cohorts than in older cohorts, although change in the older cohorts might be substantial even if it is less than change in younger cohorts. (Obviously, intercohort differences in susceptibility to change could be cohort rather than age effects.)

However, such a procedure is not always adequate by itself. Intracohort changes in percentages and in many other kinds of measures are subject to *ceiling and floor effects*, which must be taken into account in making inferences from the changes. For instance, the percentage of respondents selecting a given alternative to a question asked on a survey can never exceed 100, and in fact the effective ceiling is always somewhat less than 100, if only because a certain small percentage of survey respondents always choose "no opinion," "don't know," or whatever noncommital response alternative is offered. Likewise, there is a lower limit, since the percentage cannot be less than zero. To illustrate, suppose that at time one the percentage choosing a given alternative is 70 in one cohort and 90 in another. Suppose that the percentage in the first cohort increases by 20 points, to 90 by time two. The second cohort cannot experience a 20-point increase, since it is only 10 points from the upper limit, so its failure to show an increase equal to that in the first cohort in no sense implies that it is generally less susceptible to change.

When the upper and lower limits are such that change in one cohort cannot equal that which occurs in another cohort, the operation of ceiling or floor effects is undeniable. Under other circumstances, however, one cannot be certain whether or not ceiling or floor effects are reflected in the data. For instance, suppose that the percentages in two cohorts at time one are 60 and 80 respectively. If, in general, the two cohorts are equally susceptible to change and if they are subjected to the same stimuli, is an increase of 10 percentage points equally likely in the two cohorts? The answer is not known, and it may differ from one dependent variable to another. All we can usually say in such a case is that there is some reason to suspect a ceiling effect, although there will occasionally be empirical clues. For instance, if two cohorts change at equal rates during several periods of time, and if change in one cohort becomes smaller when it, but not the other cohort, comes within a certain range of the upper or lower limit, then a ceiling or floor effect is suggested.

Good discussions of ceiling and floor effects are rare in the social scientific literature, and they are virtually nonexistent in elementary statistics and methods textbooks. Some of the existing discussions are based on inadequate theory and evidence concerning how the effects operate. For instance, there is often no mention of the very important distinction between ceiling and floor effects which are empirical—that is, the upper and lower limits on the possible magnitude of the variable exist in the "real world"—and effects which are artifacts of the method of measurement. (An example of the first kind of effects is in the case of voter turnout, which empirically cannot exceed 100 percent or drop below zero; and an example of the second kind is in the case of tests scores on an examination on American history, for which the highest and lowest possible scores—100 and zero—do not represent empirical limits of the range of knowledge.) "Transformations" to "remove" ceiling and floor effects are often mechanically applied without adequate consideration of whether or not the effects should be "removed" or whether the transformation adequately represents the way ceiling and floor effects operate. Consequently, the cohort analyst is once again faced with a situation in which there is a clear need for "rigor" but no clearly appropriate rigorous techniques to apply. In the absence of precise knowledge of the nature of ceiling and floor effects, there of course can be no precise way to correct for them.

However, the cohort analyst can be sensitive to the possibility of ceiling and floor effects and alert to situations in which they may be present. Occasionally, these effects are rather clearly not reflected in the data. For instance, in the case of approval of admission of Communist China to the United Nations in 1954 (Table 5), the values were low and almost uniform across the cohorts, so clearly the potential for increase was about the same for all of them. Therefore, the fact that the percentages increased more in the younger cohorts than in the older ones in the following years strongly suggests that the older cohorts were less susceptible to change on this variable, either because they were older or because they had different formative experiences.

Furthermore, there are some "rigorous" methods which can be useful if they are applied and interpreted cautiously and with intelligence. In the case of studies designed to study susceptibility to change, a "correction" for ceiling or floor effects is needed regardless of whether the limits are empirical or artifactual. And a correction can be useful for some purposes even if it is not precise. For instance, if any of the cohort percentages fall below the point at which floor effects should be suspected (about 30, as a very rough rule of thumb, depending on how rapidly the percentages are trending downward), it may be useful to transform the observed percentages into their common logarithms. This transformation takes into account that as the floor is approached, movement toward it will decelerate; as the values drop toward zero, decrements of a percentage point become progressively larger on the log scale. If the deceleration due to floor effects is accurately taken into account by the logarithmic transformation, then the cohorts exhibiting the greatest change on the log scale will be those with the greatest susceptibility to change (or, possibly, the greatest exposure to stimuli for change). If the percentages are moving toward 100 rather than zero, their complements (the differences between them and 100) are used for the transformation. In other words, ceiling effects become floor effects.

This procedure is illustrated in Table 12. The data in the left side of the table are the percentages of persons in 1959 and in 1969 in five 10-year cohorts who said they would vote for a Catholic for president. The percentage increased from 1959 to 1969 in each of the cohorts, according to the data; and contrary to the hypothesis of an aging-rigidity effect, there was no apparent consistent tendency for the younger cohorts to change more than the older ones. However, since the percentage in the youngest cohort exceeded 90 in 1969 and thus was approaching the upper limit, ceiling effects may have prevented the hypothesized pattern of change. Therefore, I converted the percentages to their complements and transformed the complements to their common logarithms (right side of Table 12). The intracohort changes on the log scale fall into the hypothesized

TABLE 12

Percentage of Non-Catholic Respondents Who Said They Would Vote for a Catholic for President,[1] in Five 10-Year Birth Cohorts, 1959 and 1969

	Percentages (N)			Complements (Log)		
	1959	1969	Change	1959	1969	(Log Change)
Cohort 1--Age:	20-29	30-39		20-29	30-39	
	74.3 (174)	93.7 (243)	+19.4	25.7 (1.41)	6.3 (0.80)	(-.61)
Cohort 2--Age:	30-39	40-49		30-39	40-49	
	69.0 (223)	88.6 (212)	+19.6	31.0 (1.49)	11.4 (1.06)	(-.43)
Cohort 3--Age:	40-49	50-59		40-49	50-59	
	65.2 (238)	82.8 (136)	+17.6	34.8 (1.54)	17.2 (1.24)	(-.30)
Cohort 4--Age:	50-59	60-69		50-59	60-69	
	55.9 (202)	80.3 (171)	+24.4	44.1 (1.64)	19.7 (1.29)	(-.35)
Cohort 5--Age:	60-69	70-79		60-69	70-79	
	54.8 (177)	69.6 (114)	+14.8	45.2 (1.66)	30.4 (1.48)	(-.18)

Source: American Institute of Public Opinion (American Gallup) Surveys 622 and 776.

[1] Standardized to a sex ratio of 100.

pattern, except that the value for cohort 4 exceeds that for cohort 3. In this case, whether or not the logarithmic transformation precisely corrects for ceiling effects is not very important, since obviously a correction of any magnitude would move the intracohort changes toward the pattern predicted by the hypothesis.

CONCLUSIONS

This paper deals with only the basic and elementary concepts, logic, and techniques of cohort analysis; any cohort analyst who goes beyond the simplest study will encounter problems not discussed here. Furthermore, since cohort analysis with survey sample data is still in its infancy, most cohort analysts will encounter problems not discussed in any published literature. To a large extent, therefore, successful cohort analysis during the next few years will depend on originality, inventiveness, and ability to adapt techniques developed for other purposes to the analysis of cohort data. There is no cookbook to guide the researcher step-by-step through an analysis and interpretation of data.

In most of this paper, I emphasize specific techniques of analysis, albeit rather simple ones; and certainly a mastery of at least the simpler techniques is requisite to successful cohort analysis. However, I try to stress that application of any of the techniques and interpretation of any cohort data require good grounding in the relevant theory plus knowledge of a wide range of "side information" from outside the cohort table. I do not try here to teach recent history, theories of social and cultural change, theories of adult development, or theories of political behavior; however, depending on the purpose of the research and the background of the researcher, several days to several weeks of reading on some or all of these topics should precede any cohort study. Successful cohort analysis with nondemographic dependent variables depends at least as much on knowledge of these topics as on technical expertise.

NOTES

1. For discussion of the confounding of age, cohort, and period effects, I draw indirectly (without quoting or paraphrasing) on Mason, Mason, Winsborough, and Poole (1973), and Riley, Johnson, and Foner (1972).

2. Assumption 3 may seem inconsistent with the fact that a 10-point reduction in percentage of conservatives occurred at each age level. However, that change was due to both period influences and cohort succession, and cohort succession accounted for more of the change at the older age levels—an illustration of the complexity of cohort data.

3. Converse (1976) aptly refers to these elements as "side information," a term I use frequently.

4. However, the Gallup data gathered prior to 1942 are not ideal for cohort analysis, since age was estimated by the interviewer rather than reported by the respondent. Unfortunately, data gathered by the other major polling organizations during the 1930s and 1940s are rarely useful for cohort analysis, since age was coded into broad categories of unequal size.

5. Some reports of cohort studies refer briefly to similar data for other countries, but to my knowledge, none systematically compares data from two or more countries.

6. Although Sudman and Bradburn (1974) deal with what I call "response bias," they prefer not to use that term.

7. However, as Converse (1976) points out, even the best national samples do not adequately represent young adults under age 25. Therefore, any observed differences between persons under age 25 and older persons should be interpreted with caution.

8. Simple random sampling is used only if population size varies little among the areas. Usually, a kind of sampling which takes into account the unequal sizes of the clusters must be used (see Kish, 1965).

9. However, the variation by age will not be as steep as that shown in Table 7.

10. Conversely, researchers who concentrate on explained variance often "under-interpret" important associations.

11. Additional evidence that the age variation in independence at the four dates covered by the study reflects almost entirely the effects of aging is that the data closely approximate the pattern predicted by pure age effects (see Table 7). The level of independence remained virtually constant in the entire adult population, whereas in the absence of offsetting period or compositional effects, any important cohort effects would have increased the level of independence during the 12-year period (see Table 8). Obviously, if I had followed my own advice to begin any cohort study with a search for patterns of variation predicted by pure effects, I would have arrived at a different conclusion.

On the other hand, evidence that the 1945-1957 pattern of age variation in independence reflects largely age effects is not definitive. Paul Abramson (in personal correspondence) argues that examination of data for *whites alone* suggests greater cohort differences in independence than does Converse's study (see Abramson, 1976). Furthermore, everyone who has written on the topic (or at least Abramson, Converse, and myself) apparently agrees that the steep age differences in independence which emerged in the late 1960s are largely intercohort differences rather than effects of aging.

12. If the numbers of cases in the cells should be equal, if the values in the cells should be means on an interval scale, and if the respondents should be evenly distributed within the broad age levels, regression analyses performed on data in each row and in each column would yield inter-row and inter-column variation only in the intercepts, or constant terms, not in the correlation or regression coefficients.

13. A possible example is in U.S. national data which show that a negative association of reported happiness with age in the late 1950s and early 1960s had been replaced by a weak positive relationship by the early 1970s (NORC data in the author's files). Instead of reflecting nonlinear cohort effects, this age-period interaction may well reflect a change in age effects.

REFERENCES

ABRAMSON, P. R. (1976) "Generational change and the decline of party identification in America, 1952-1974." Amer. Pol. Sci. Rev. (June): 469-478.
——— (1975) Generational Change in American Politics. Lexington, Mass.: D. C. Heath.
——— (1974) "Generational change in American electoral behavior." Amer. Pol. Sci. Rev. (March): 93-105.
BALTES, P. B. and G. REINERT (1969) "Cohort effects in cognitive development of children as revealed by cross-sectional sequences." Developmental Psychology (September): 169-177.
BLALOCK, H. M., Jr. (1972) Social Statistics. 2nd. ed. New York: McGraw-Hill.
——— (1967) "Status inconsistency, social mobility, status integration and structural effects." Amer. Soc. Rev. (October): 790-801.
——— (1966) "The identification problem and theory building: the case of status inconsistency." Amer. Soc. Rev. (February): 52-61.
BOTWINICK, J. (1973) Aging and Behavior. New York: Springer.
CARLSSON, G. and K. KARLSSON (1970) "Age, cohorts and the generation of generations." Amer. Soc. Rev. (August): 710-718.
CONVERSE, P. E. (1976) The Dynamics of Party Identification. Beverly Hills and London: Sage Pub.
CRITTENDEN, J. (1963) "Aging and political participation." Western Political Q. (June): 323-331.
——— (1962) "Aging and party affiliation." Public Opinion Q. (Winter): 648-657.
CUMMING, E. and W. E. HENRY (1961) Growing Old. New York: Basic Books.
CUTLER, N. (1970) "Generation, maturation, and party affiliation: a cohort analysis." Public Opinion Q. (Winter): 583-591.
——— (1968) The Alternative Effects of Generations and Aging Upon Political Behavior: A Cohort Analysis of American Attitudes Toward Foreign Policy, 1946-1966. Oak Ridge, Tenn.: Oak Ridge National Lab.
——— and V. L. BENGTSON (1974) "Age and political alienation: maturation, generation and period effects." Annals of the Amer. Academy of Pol. and Soc. Science (September): 160-175.
CUTLER, S. J. and R. L. KAUFMAN (1975) "Cohort changes in political attitudes: tolerance of ideological nonconformity." Public Opinion Q. (Spring): 68-81.
GALLUP, G. (1972) The Gallup Poll: Public Opinion, 1935-1971. New York: Random House.
GLENN, N. D. (1975a) "Psychological well-being in the postparental stage: some evidence from national surveys." J. of Marriage and the Family (February): 105-110.
——— (1975b) "Trend studies with available survey data: opportunities and pitfalls," pp. 6-48 in Social Science Research Council, Survey Data for Trend Analysis: An Index to Repeated Questions in U.S. National Surveys Held by the Roper Public Opinion Research Center. Williamstown, Mass.: Roper Center.
——— (1974) "Aging and conservatism." Annals of the Amer. Academy of Pol. and Soc. Science (September): 176-186.
——— (1972) "Sources of the shift to political independence: some evidence from a cohort analysis." Social Science Q. (December): 494-519.
——— (1970) "Problems of comparability in trend studies with opinion poll data." Public Opinion Q. (Spring): 82-91.

GLENN, N. D. and M. D. GRIMES (1968) "Aging, voting, and political interest." Amer. Soc. Rev. (August): 563-575.

GLENN, N. D. and T. HEFNER (1972) "Further evidence on aging and party identification." Public Opinion Q. (Spring): 31-47.

GLENN, N. D. and R. E. ZODY (1970) "Cohort analysis with national survey data." Gerontologist (Autumn): 233-240.

GLENN, N. D., P. A. TAYLOR, and C. H. WEAVER (1977) "Age and job satisfaction among males and females: a multivariate, multisurvey study." J. of Applied Psychology (April).

GOODMAN, L. A. (1972) "A general model for the analysis of surveys." Amer. J. of Sociology (May): 1035-1086.

HENKEL, R. E. (1976) Tests of Significance. Sage University Papers series on Quantitative Applications in the Social Sciences, 07-004. Beverly Hills and London: Sage Pub.

HOUT, M. and D. KNOKE (1975) "Change in voter turnout, 1952-1972." Public Opinion Q. (Spring): 52-68.

HYMAN, H. H. (1972) Secondary Analysis of Sample Surveys: Principles, Procedures and Potentialities. New York: John Wiley.

IVERSEN, G. R. and H. NORPOTH (1976) Analysis of Variance. Sage University Papers series on Quantitative Applications in the Social Sciences, 07-001. Beverly Hills and London: Sage Pub.

JENCKS, C. (1972) Inequality: A reassessment of the Effects of Family and Schooling in America. New York: Basic Books.

KISH, L. (1965) Survey Sampling. New York: John Wiley.

KNOKE, D. and M. HOUT (1974) "Social and demographic factors in American political party affiliations, 1952-72." Amer. Soc. Rev. (October): 700-713.

MANNHEIM, K. (1928) Essays in the Sociology of Knowledge. London: Routeledge & Kegan Paul.

MASON, K. O., W. MASON, H. H. WINSBOROUGH, and W. K. POOLE (1973) "Some methodological issues in the cohort analysis of archival data." Amer. Soc. Rev. (April): 242-258.

NEWMAN, K. (1975) AIPO Surveys: To Weight or Not to Weight. (mimeo) Chicago: National Opinion Research Center.

PALMORE, E. and F. C. JEFFERS (1971) Prediction of Life Span. Lexington, Mass.: D. C. Heath.

RILEY, M. W. (1973) "Aging and cohort succession: interpretations and misinterpretations." Public Opinion Q. (Spring): 35-49.

——— M. JOHNSON, and ANNE FONER (1972) Aging and Society, Vol. 3: A Sociology of Age Stratification. New York: Russell Sage Foundation.

RYDER, N. B. (1965) "The cohort as a concept in the study of social change." Amer. Soc. Rev. (December): 843-361.

SCHAIE, K. W. and C. R. STROTHER (1968a) "A cross-sequential study of age changes in cognitive behavior." Psychological Bull. (December): 671-680.

——— (1968b) "The effect of time and cohort differences on the interpretation of age changes in cognitive behavior." Multivariate Behavioral Research (July): 259-293.

Social Science Research Council (1975) Survey Data for Trend Analysis: An Index of Repeated Questions in U.S. National Surveys Held by the Roper Public Opinion Research Center. Williamstown, Mass.: Roper Center.

STEPHAN, F. F. and P. J. McCARTHY (1958) Sampling Opinions. New York: John Wiley.

SUDMAN, S. and N. M. BRADBURN (1974) Response Effects in Surveys. Chicago: Aldine.

USLANER, E. M. (forthcoming) Regression Analysis: Simultaneous Equation Estimation. In this series of Sage University Papers in Quantitative Applications in the Social Sciences.

WHYTE, W. H., Jr. (1956) The Organization Man. New York: Simon & Schuster.

WILLIAMS, J. A., Jr. (1968) "Interviewer role performance: a further note on bias in the information interview." Public Opinion Q. (Summer): 287-294.

——— (1964) "Interviewer-respondent interaction: a study of bias in the information interview." Sociometry (September): 338-352.

WINGROVE, C. R. and J. P. ALSTON (1974) "Cohort analysis of church attendance, 1939-69." Social Forces (December): 324-331.

DATE DUE

Glenn   163143